D0899092

6/25/13
#21.50

JIM GARRISON'S
BOURBON STREET BRAWL

THE MAKING OF A FIRST AMENDMENT MILESTONE

Jim Garrison's Bourbon Street Brawl

The Making of a First Amendment Milestone

James Savage

University of Louisiana at Lafayette Press
2010

PHOTO CREDITS: Garrison on Bourbon Street and the U.S. Supreme Court, courtesy of the Associated Press; the five nightclubs, courtesy of The Historic New Orleans Collection; Garrison on surveillance and the Orleans Parish Criminal District Court, from *Saturday Evening Post*; Jack P. F. Gremillion, courtesy of the Louisiana State Supreme Court Library; Norma Wallace, from *New Orleans Magazine*; and Jim Garrison, courtesy of the New Orleans Public Library.

http://ulpress.org
University of Louisiana at Lafayette Press
P.O. Box 40831
Lafayette, LA 70504-0831

Printed on acid-free paper.

ISBN 13 (paper): 978-1-887366-95-3
ISBN 10 (paper): 1-887366-95-4

Library of Congress Cataloging-in-Publication Data

Savage, James A.
Jim Garrison's Bourbon Street brawl : the making of a First Amendment milestone / James Savage.
    p. cm.
Includes bibliographical references and index.
ISBN-13: 978-1-887366-95-3 (pbk. : alk. paper)
ISBN-10: 1-887366-95-4 (pbk. : alk. paper)
1. Garrison, Jim, 1921-1992--Trials, litigation, etc. 2. Trials (Libel)--Louisiana--New Orleans. 3. Freedom of speech--United States. 4. United States. Constitution. 1st Amendment. 5. United States. Supreme Court. 6. Shaw, Clay, 1912?- 7. Kennedy, John F. (John Fitzgerald), 1917-1963--Assassination. I. Title.
    KF224.G3775S38 2010
    342.7308'53--dc22
                        2010003496

Table of Contents

Acknowledgements

After writing nearly one hundred and fifty pages on a Supreme Court case, a simple listing of those to whom I feel indebted should be easy.

It is not.

Do not let the name on this book fool you—this is not the work of just one person, and it is with the deepest gratitude that I recognize the exceptional individuals whose names belong next to my own. Merely listing them does not seem an adequate expression of my thanks, but here it goes anyway.

The staffs at the various archival facilities that I visited or contacted never ignored my e-mails or failed to bring out yet another box, even when I had sifted through it before. These wonderful professionals include Lia Apodaca, Manuscript Division, Library of Congress; Jennifer Cole, Seeley G. Mudd Manuscript Library, Princeton University; Addy Sonder and Michael Widener, Rare Books & Special Collections, Tarlton Law Library, University of Texas at Austin; the Clerk of Court's staff and the librarians at the Louisiana Supreme Court; and James Mathis, National Archives and Records Administration.

My thanks also to Hugo L. Black Jr. for granting access to his father's papers at the Library of Congress, and to Kelly Chew and David Heller at the Media Law Resource Center, who generously provided copies of MLRC publications concerning developments in criminal defamation law.

The University of Louisiana at Lafayette was the cradle for *Jim Garrison's Bourbon Street Brawl*, both in its early incarnation as my master's thesis and now as a book. I owe no small debt to my thesis committee, chaired by the extraordinary Dr. Mary Farmer-Kaiser, who pushed me throughout my graduate school career and who continues to do so, even from a distance. She is not only my mentor, but she is also my friend. The committee's remaining members, Dr. Michael Martin and Dr. Vaughan Baker, never failed to open their doors for consultations, both professional and personal, during my graduate school tenure. I am fortunate to have had their exacting pens pass over these pages.

Drs. Farmer-Kaiser, Martin, and Baker each encouraged me to submit the thesis to the University of Louisiana at Lafayette Press, where it has further benefited from the wisdom and patience of James Wilson, Jessica Hornbuckle, and Katherine Dankert. Anthony Miller, my colleague at the University of Kentucky, dedicated several weeks of his summer vacation to reading the manuscript. I thank him for his comments and enthusiasm, and I thank his wife, Stephanie, for being Stephanie.

Equally as important to this project was the support of my family: my mother, Carol Morrow Savage; my father and stepmother, Dan and Ann Savage; my sister Danielle; and my sisters and brothers-in-law, Traci and Joey Melancon, and Ashley and Billy Lacobie.

Finally, my sisters and their husbands have given me the best gift for which I could ask—six loving, devoted, and charismatic children without whom my life would be very boring. In their short lives, they have already learned the art of self-expression, and I know others will come to appreciate their opinions as I have. So, to Kaitie, Peter, Abby, James Quinn, Ellie, and Owen, I leave you with this. You have been endowed with the gift of speech and the capacity for free thought. The world can move—or not—depending on how you chose to use them. It is to you and to your futures that this book is lovingly dedicated.

Introduction

Garrison v. Louisiana: The Case of the "Jolly Green Giant" and the First Amendment

By November 1964, Jim Garrison had served eighteen months as New Orleans' district attorney. Garrison's rise from the obscure post of assistant city prosecutor to the position of the parish's top lawyer had been unlikely—he was the first district attorney to take office without allegiance to an organized political machine. In less than two years, however, Garrison became arguably the most powerful politician in New Orleans and, perhaps, in the state of Louisiana. The fact that Garrison owed his dominance of the city's political landscape to the Supreme Court of the United States was as improbable as his rise to notoriety.[1]

Bourbon Street prostitutes, eight criminal court judges, and the district attorney's acid tongue brought Garrison to the Supreme Court's attention in the spring of 1964. Shortly after becoming district attorney in May 1962, Garrison engaged in a public feud with the parish's criminal court judges over funding for his office. The district attorney claimed that financial limitations the judges had imposed were a concerted effort to halt his ongoing campaign against vice in the city's French Quarter. He charged that the monetary restrictions raised "interesting questions about the racketeer influences" on the judges, whom he had described earlier as "sacred cows." Based on those statements and a litany of others, the jurists successfully sued Garrison for criminal defamation, and he appealed his conviction to the U.S. Supreme Court.[2]

During an eight-month period between March and November 1964, the U.S. Supreme Court issued two rulings that redefined the nation's libel laws. The first was *New York Times v. Sullivan*; the second, *Garrison v. Louisiana*. In overturning Garrison's defamation conviction, the court confronted for the first time the contradiction between state criminal libel laws and the First Amendment's free speech protections. In the *Times* case, the justices had constructed a standard by which courts could measure civil libel suits; the *Times* rule granted constitutional immunity to statements made without actual malice,

1

which the court defined as "knowledge that [the statement] was false or with reckless disregard whether it was false or not." Writing for the court in *Garrison v. Louisiana*, Associate Justice William J. Brennan Jr. insisted that the *Times* civil libel standard also embraced criminal libel charges. Furthermore, Brennan characterized the right to criticize public officials as "the essence of self-government" and fundamental to democracy. In *Garrison v. Louisiana*, the court unambiguously stated that the First Amendment protected unpopular and controversial speech and limited the government's ability to utilize defamation laws to suppress statements critical of its conduct.[3]

With these sweeping pronouncements, the Supreme Court elevated the *Garrison* case from a financial and political dispute between an upstart district attorney and a group of inveterate judges to a First Amendment milestone that strengthened the fundamental right of free speech in the United States. In addition to its significance nationwide, the decision also held local implications for Jim Garrison. The district attorney's feud with the judges strengthened his political prestige in both New Orleans and statewide and allowed Garrison to cultivate a public image as an independent, reform-minded prosecutor fighting an entrenched machine system. In actuality, Garrison's desire to upend the city's existing political structure and to expand his own influence inspired the malevolence from which the case of *Garrison v. Louisiana* emanated. While significant for its expansion of free speech, the Supreme Court's decision allowed Garrison to cement his dominance of New Orleans' political landscape. With few now willing to challenge him, Garrison was free to do as he wished—even to investigate a presidential murder with tenuous ties to his jurisdiction.

In 1967, three years after the Supreme Court ruled in *Garrison v. Louisiana*, the district attorney announced his own inquiry into the assassination of President John F. Kennedy. Over the ensuing four decades, historians, other scholars, and amateur sleuths have dissected Garrison's Kennedy probe, which culminated in his failed 1969 conspiracy prosecution of New Orleans business executive Clay L. Shaw. Admittedly, this contentious field of study has merit; Garrison remains the only public official in the United States to challenge in court the official story of Kennedy's death. The countless books, documentaries, periodicals, and motion picture portrayals of the Shaw prosecution invariably mention Garrison's early efforts to clean up New Orleans vice and his subsequent tussle with the judges, but few chronicle what happened when the case moved off Bourbon Street and into the nation's highest court. Even fewer have explored the significance of *Garrison v. Louisiana* to Garrison's career and, more important, the case's role in expanding the right of free speech in the United States.

This book provides the information missing from previous accounts of Garrison's life and career. It is therefore not another exploration of his Kennedy inquiry; the focus here is *Garrison v. Louisiana*. Although the assassination probe propelled Garrison to international stature in 1967, his Bourbon Street raids, row with the judges, and subsequent defamation conviction five years earlier brought him the first national attention of his career. Reporters flocked to the maverick, crusading district attorney who dared to confront the entrenched political establishment of one of the South's largest cities. The *Washington Post, New York Times, Newsweek, Saturday Evening Post,* and *National Observer* carried flattering stories about Garrison's escapades. These press accounts were glowing, almost hagiographic, and a man of Garrison's immense ego could not have asked for a better introduction to a nationwide audience. The news articles demonstrated Garrison's flair for literary illusion, his penchant for puncturing reputations, and the fear he inspired in others. Once, when Victor H. Schiro, New Orleans' notoriously indecisive mayor, waffled on a pressing problem, Garrison issued a press release that began, "Not since Hamlet tried to decide whether or not to stab the Prince of Denmark has there been such agonizing over a political decision." On another occasion, Garrison summarized the prosecutorial record of predecessor Richard Dowling by characterizing the former district attorney as "the great emancipator—he let everybody go free." Few chose to tangle with Garrison, as Louisiana Governor John J. McKeithen once told an out-of-state newspaper reporter: "I have learned that most of Garrison's enemies are dead—politically speaking—and I don't want to join the list of the deceased," the governor conceded.[4]

While reporters captured Garrison's charisma and political prowess, they struggled with the duality of his personality; one journalist perceptively characterized the prosecutor as "a puzzle." He was indeed—but it was a puzzle of Garrison's own making. In an age before the American political lexicon redefined the word "spin," Garrison exhibited a remarkable, almost mystical ability to manipulate his public image. In the case of his row with the judges, the prosecutor took what was essentially a fight over money and recast it as a battle for the First Amendment. A man of great magnetism, Garrison cultivated reporters and, speaking to them in his sonorous, beautifully modulated voice, reshaped reality. A journalist who covered Garrison during his Kennedy investigation characterized him as "Merlin," adding that the district attorney "draws you into his never-never land world where everything is upside down, and you get the magical sense of a total reversal of reality." Indeed, the personality traits Garrison exhibited during his assassination inquiry, including his manipulation of fact for his own benefit, were the same enigmatic qualities he displayed when the national media first discovered him during his fight with the judges five years earlier.[5]

Garrison's ability to contradict reality reflected the dichotomous nature of his own character. He was personally shy, yet his immense physical presence—his six feet, six inches, two hundred and sixty pounds earned him the moniker the "jolly green giant"—made Garrison the center of attention the minute he entered a room. He portrayed himself as a protector of the First Amendment, yet viciously attacked those who dared to criticize him. Garrison launched a campaign against commercialized vice on Bourbon Street, yet regularly frequented the nightclubs himself. He was an immaculate dresser, yet his biggest base of support was from the city's poorest residents. He professed a desire to defend the rights of individuals, yet one New Orleans newspaper described his prosecution of Clay Shaw as "a perversion of the legal process as has not been often seen." Finally, as the origins of *Garrison v. Louisiana* demonstrate, the prosecutor cultivated the image of a crusader fighting against the city's establishment while he covertly worked to expand his own political power.[6]

Like its namesake, the case of *Garrison v. Louisiana* is in itself a contradiction, one with which the U.S. Supreme Court grappled during their deliberations. The case's underlying malevolence concerned the justices; how could they use what was essentially a parochial political fight over money and power to expand the fundamental right of free speech? Garrison's continuous public derision toward the Orleans judges, which extended well into his trial, was an obvious attempt by an upstart prosecutor to topple the city's existing political structure through ridicule. Only after his conviction, when the case moved into the appellate process, did Garrison and his attorneys shed their scornful strategy and reformulate the case based on constitutional questions. From the time the Louisiana Supreme Court considered the appeal in May 1963 until the U.S. Supreme Court issued its decision in November 1964, the case ceased to concern money and power—it became instead about the place of dissent in a democracy and the right of individuals to criticize elected officials without fear of retribution. Although Garrison would use the decision to cement the political influence he craved, the case's most abiding significance was its expansion of free speech in the United States.

Because *Garrison v. Louisiana* has not received the type of historical scrutiny the *Times* decision has, source material for this project was abundant and largely untouched.[7] For instance, at the National Archives in Washington, D.C., Supreme Court files remained tied together and packed away for four decades. A helpful archivist cheerfully cut the string, which allowed access to pieces of the neglected story. Some resources were easier to access. Local and national media reports provided colorful accounts of Garrison's Bourbon Street raids, his feud with the judges, and the district attorney's subsequent trial. Files of the Metropolitan Crime Commission, a New Orleans watchdog group, and the Records of the U.S. Supreme Court, housed respectively at National Archives facilities in College Park, Maryland and Washington, D.C., were instrumental in filling in information the press coverage lacked. New Orleans journalists Rosemary James and Jack Wardlaw and attorney Milton E. Brener authored books early in Garrison's Kennedy probe that briefly address the prosecutor's first years in office. James and Wardlaw wrote *Plot or Politics?* from the perspectives of two longtime courthouse insiders well aware of Garrison's colorful exploits after he became district attorney. Brener was among the first staff members Garrison hired after he assumed office in May 1962. Brener's book, *The Garrison Case,* like *Plot or Politics?*, focuses on the Kennedy probe, but delivers keen observances of the inner workings of the prosecutor's office early in Garrison's term.

Furthermore, the trial transcript, available in its entirety in the *Records and Briefs* microfiche series, supplemented newspaper coverage of the court proceedings. The invaluable *Records and Briefs* series also contained the entire case file sent to the U.S. Supreme Court after it consented to review Garrison's appeal. In New Orleans, the microfilmed records of the Louisiana Supreme Court and the files of the Orleans Parish Criminal District Court illuminated the lower court proceedings and the beginnings of the appeals process. These documents, which were not included in the *Records and Briefs* file, illustrate how Garrison's defense team and the state prosecutors constructed the opposing arguments from which a First Amendment landmark eventually emerged.[8]

The project's explication of deliberations before the U.S. Supreme Court encompasses the widest array of sources. Again, the *Records and Briefs* microfiche collection contained the litigants' written arguments to the U.S. Supreme Court, while recordings of oral arguments from the National Archives offered a window into the courtroom both times the justices heard Garrison's appeal. More significantly, the files of seven of the nine justices on the court at the time it considered *Garrison v. Louisiana* provide a remarkable view into the tribunal's inner workings. This mass of material—collected from the Library of Congress, the University of Texas' Tarlton Law Library, and Princeton University's Seeley G. Mudd Manuscript Library—demonstrates the court's difficulty in deciding Garrison's appeal. The justices considered the *Garrison* case twice, once during its October 1963 session and again the following term. Over a six-month period, nearly thirty drafts circulated between chambers, including the majority opinion, several concurring opinions, and a number of unpublished dissents. When combined with memoranda, notes, and other correspondence, the justices' files contain more than a thousand pages of pertinent documents that reveal the disharmony among the court's members as they worked to reach a consensus opinion. In addition, one justice left handwritten notes of the court's private negotiations concerning the *Garrison* case. These notes provide an extraordinary look into secret conference room discussions, and portray the court as divided as to the merits of Garrison's appeal.[9]

The scholarship of several preeminent legal scholars offered guidance in understanding this mass of court documents. The works of Clifton O. Lawhorne, Thomas L. Tedford, Ronald Naquin, and Thomas I. Emerson proved especially helpful in understanding the impact of *New York Times v. Sullivan*, *Garrison v. Louisiana*, and subsequent cases on libel law in the United States. However, none of this scholarship focuses solely on the *Garrison* case and most portray it as less important than the earlier *Times* decision, an assertion this book disputes. Other secondary sources proved less helpful. In their examinations of Garrison's assassination inquiry, several writers, notably James DiEugenio, Patricia Lambert, and Joan Mellen, give only cursory mention to the Supreme Court case.[10]

Admittedly, there are holes in this work's primary source base. Other than press releases, Garrison left no personal reflections on the momentous Supreme Court decision that bore his name. After the 1966 launch of his Kennedy probe, Garrison became monomaniacal. The assassination obsessed him. One needs look no further than Garrison's personal files, which his family donated to the National Archives after his death in 1992, to reach this conclusion. Long after he left the district attorney's office, Garrison sorted through the files of his Kennedy inquiry year after year, annotating the documents with a date each time he rearranged them. His papers contain only one item that refers marginally to the Supreme Court case—a play Garrison wrote that features two business executives discussing the Bourbon Street raids and the judges' opposition to the crusading prosecutor's efforts. Garrison also wrote two nonfiction books and a novel after he failed to win a conviction in the Shaw case. All three works depict presidential assassinations, both real and fictional. Although these sources provided little assistance, the ever-loquacious Garrison fortunately made hundreds of statements to the local and national press during the two-year span this project describes.[11]

These sources form the basis of what is to date the most-extensive explication of *Garrison v. Louisiana*. Researched for nearly two years, this project has reshaped my own feelings about the decision and about Garrison himself. My early writings on the case portrayed Garrison as colorful, charming, and clever—a breed of politician that Louisiana had exported to the world before ethics laws and federal grand juries stunted behavior engrained in the region's political fabric. With more investigation, however, I realized I had fallen under Garrison's spell. More than a decade after his death, the prosecutor manipulated me as he had manipulated so many reporters and voters four decades earlier. I began to labor under the belief that Garrison indeed was guilty of defaming the judges. He meant to injure their reputations and when the jurists filed charges against him, he hid behind the First Amendment. That fact alone assaulted my firm belief in the preeminence of the right of free speech and of the press. The idea that Garrison misled the U.S. Supreme Court further enflamed my moral outrage—until it occurred to me that the nation's highest court cared less about the circumstances of Garrison's trial than it did the law under which he was prosecuted. As a result, it became less important to me to prove either Garrison's guilt or innocence. I chose instead to demonstrate why the case, even with shady underpinnings that allowed Garrison to consolidate his local influence, stands today as a significant expansion of First Amendment rights.

In the introduction to his 1988 memoir, *On the Trail of the Assassins,* Garrison displayed characteristic self-aggrandizement when he mused that, despite his failed conspiracy prosecution of Clay Shaw, many of his theories concerning the Kennedy assassination had withstood the intense scrutiny of armchair detectives and congressional investigators alike. "History has a way of changing verdicts," Garrison reflected, asking rhetorically, "Clarence Darrow lost the Scopes trial, but who remembers that now?" One might say the same about Jim Garrison himself. Unlike Darrow, however, history remembers Garrison not for the case he won but for the one he lost. His forgotten victory, *Garrison v. Louisiana,* was more than a legal and political triumph for an individual. The decision's enhancement of free speech far exceeds the local ramifications the case held for Garrison's political career. Furthermore, the case raised issues about the right of free expression and the place of criticism in a democracy that continue to resonate.[12]

Chapter I

Born on Bourbon Street:
A Landmark's Shady Beginnings

In August 1962, less than two months after he became New Orleans' district attorney, Jim Garrison began a series of well-publicized raids on Bourbon Street, the city's gaudy strip of adult entertainment venues. These were nothing new. Many past district attorneys and police superintendents had attempted to stymie the vice, prostitution, and other nefarious deeds for which Bourbon Street was notorious. Some locals expected Garrison's raids to go exactly where all the others had—nowhere. "Listen, dear," famed madam Norma Wallace told a *Saturday Evening Post* reporter in 1963, "I've seen DA's become ex-DA's and police chiefs become ex-police chiefs, and mayors become ex-mayors. But I've never become an ex-madam." An unnamed observer predicted that Garrison would peak early and then would embrace the status quo, just as others had before him. "In this town, a reformer is just an outsider who wants to get in on the inside," the anonymous commentator reflected, continuing, "So he hoots and hollers and wins office—and gets gentled down."[1]

Garrison's raids differed from his predecessors' fruitless efforts, however. The district attorney forced the closure of a dozen nightclubs that peddled sex and overpriced liquor to tourists. More important, the anti-vice operations pitted him against eight Orleans Parish judges. When the jurists limited Garrison's expenditures for his vice operations, he implied they were under the influence of racketeers, and the judges promptly charged the prosecutor with defamation. The U.S. Supreme Court would eventually overturn Garrison's conviction in a case that broadened an individual's right to criticize public officials without fear of criminal prosecution.[2]

Bourbon Street thus became the birthplace of *Garrison v. Louisiana*, a landmark for First Amendment rights, and Garrison used the victory to consolidate his political power and to bolster his image as a defender of free speech. "The Bill of Rights . . . lives in a kind of oxygen tent," he told Tulane University law students in late 1964, after the Supreme Court reversed his conviction, "and a twenty-four hour

9

watch is needed because someone is always turning off the oxygen—always in the interest of justice, of course." Despite the district attorney's claims, *Garrison v. Louisiana* was not the result of a crusading prosecutor fighting judges who unconscionably supported pimps and racketeers, nor was it merely a vigorous defense of free speech. In fact, the case had decidedly ignoble origins. Garrison's desire to eliminate the financial controls the judges held over his office fueled a barrage of dishonest and malicious statements aimed at damaging the reputations of those who opposed him. For Garrison, ever distrustful of political power held by others, the feud with the judges had the added advantage of allowing him to challenge the entrenched New Orleans political establishment and to widen his own influence in the process. Therefore, Garrison's later insistence that his confrontation with the judges was a battle for the sanctity of free speech was yet another manifestation of the dishonesty he had used to consolidate his political power. Money, animosity, and deception were the real foundations of this First Amendment milestone.[3]

Bourbon Street seems an unlikely place to find the origins of a landmark Supreme Court decision, but it is among the strip clubs and honkytonks of New Orleans' adult entertainment district that the roots of *Garrison v. Louisiana* lie. Beginning in early August 1962, Garrison initiated raids and undercover investigations of at least two dozen nightspots. One such investigation took place on the night of November 26, 1962, when plain-clothes agents Warren Moity and Theodore de la Houssaye entered Jazz Ltd., a Bourbon Street nightclub, and took a table near the club's rear. Tanya "Jackel" Sanchez and Theresa "Dixie" Selensky soon approached the table, sat down, and asked the pair to buy them a bottle of champagne. In exchange, the women offered to pleasure the two men sexually. In an hour's time, Moity spent $215 and complained to the waiter that he had not received change after paying for each bottle of champagne. "Don't worry about money," Selensky told Moity, "pay the man and you'll enjoy yourself." A few nights later, on November 30 at around 4 a.m., Moity and de la Houssaye returned to Jazz Ltd., with a third friend, Malcolm Dodge, in tow. A waiter escorted the trio to a darkened back booth where several women joined them. The women again asked the men to buy champagne, and as Moity paid for each bottle, the waiter never

returned any change. As in the previous visit, the women proposi-
tioned the men. "They talked to us about sex the whole time we were
sitting at the table," Dodge later said. The following night, based on
information the three informants provided, the District Attorney's
Office arrested five of Jazz Ltd.'s employees, including Selensky and
Sanchez. They joined twenty other women and eight men arrested
the same night during raids on clubs that the district attorney's plain-
clothes agents had infiltrated over the preceding week.[4]

As vice arrests mounted, so did the cost. The District Attorney's
Office supplied its plain-clothes investigators with cash for their undercover work, but without receipts to prove how they spent the money, reimbursement became increasingly difficult. State law required
the district attorney to provide documentation of expenditures to an
Orleans Parish Criminal District Court judge for approval. Since August, the District Attorney's Office staff and its police investigators
had raided dozens of clubs lining Bourbon and Canal streets for sus-
picion of B-drinking, a scheme in which club owners instructed their
female employees to use sex to entice male customers into buying
overpriced liquor. Garrison maintained that this practice resulted in
the extortion of hundreds of dollars from male bar patrons and led to
prostitution. In a B-drinking swindle, club owners instructed dancers
or waitresses to approach a male customer and ask him to purchase
her a drink. If the customer agreed, the woman invited him to a booth
in the rear of the club. A *Washington Post* reporter explained how the
scheme progressed: "During the party, champagne at $30 a bottle gets
you all kinds of promises and, sometimes, a little more than promises."
As the drinking continued and the unwitting "mark" became more in-
toxicated, the waiters stopped bringing change. Eventually, the man's
money was gone—and so was the woman. Club personnel escorted,
sometimes forcibly, the now-penniless, drunken man to the door. The
scheme played out night after night throughout the summer and fall as
Garrison's investigators infiltrated clubs and left hundreds of dollars
behind. The raids "were expensive," the *Washington Post* commented,
"because Bourbon Street is expensive." As arrests mounted—the district attorney jailed more than one hundred in the operation's first
week alone—Garrison continued to incur expenses as he employed
more undercover investigators and planned more raids.[5]

By late 1962, the district attorney cited twenty-four clubs that regularly engaged in B-drinking scams and other vice violations. Early the next year, his office padlocked a dozen of these nightspots. "I don't think there is going to be a single strip joint left by early spring," Garrison told a September meeting of French Quarter property owners, who earlier had issued a public statement applauding the prosecutor's efforts "to make Bourbon [Street] obey the law." Civic groups and the press continued to praise Garrison's campaign. The *New Orleans Times-Picayune* characterized the French Quarter as "a good, green valley" tarnished by the presence of "punks and prostitutes." The crackdown, the newspaper suggested, drove "out of the shadows that edge the garish neon strip the thugs who menace residents and tourists." In a letter to Garrison, the watchdog Metropolitan Crime Commission claimed the district attorney's assault eradicated the "pseudo-respectability and a false sense of immunity from the law" long enjoyed by certain nightclub owners, gamblers, and pimps. The operation drew less enthusiastic responses from others in New Orleans, however. A cab driver, concerned about the raids' effect on the city's tourist trade, told an out-of-town journalist, "They gotta stop that guy before he turns New Orleans into a Des Moines." A New Orleans newspaper reporter took a more philosophical position. "The nice people in the quarter look upon [Bourbon Street] as a sort of sister with an indiscreet past," he commented, continuing, "She may not be respectable, but she still belongs to the family." Garrison ignored the complaints as he reveled in the favorable headlines and commendations.[6]

As the public debated the merits of the vice cleanup, the district attorney encountered financial limitations imposed by the parish's eight criminal court judges. In late August, the judges informed Garrison they would restrict further payments for his vice investigations. The jurists and the district attorney agreed that they could devise a better system for expenditures, and money issues did not seem to faze the district attorney that autumn. He issued no public complaints about the lack of funds and secured a personal bank loan to continue his operations until he and the judges could establish new financial guidelines. Garrison was not the only one feeling a financial squeeze; nightly raids and mounting arrests also lightened the pocketbooks of

Bourbon Street's proprietors and showgirls. "I don't know why Garrison is doing this to us," one club owner complained in early 1963, insisting, "I run a clean place, not a brothel. Business is down forty percent since he went on his rampage." He concluded, "Bourbon Street is one of the biggest tourist attractions in town, and without tourists, this town will go dead." Police in Lake Charles, Louisiana, discovered at least six former New Orleans strippers hitchhiking through town one weekend in late August. "New Orleans isn't a good spot for girls working bars anymore," one of them reportedly told authorities, who promptly escorted the women to the city line and urged them to continue their trek to Texas. In early September, a New Orleans civil court judge denied a petition from several club proprietors to enjoin the District Attorney's Office from conducting further raids. Later that month, a number of Bourbon Street clubs temporarily locked their doors in a coordinated protest; many threatened to stage a similar closure the following year during the American Legion's national convention to demonstrate the amount of tourism revenue they generated for the city.[7]

An odor of hypocrisy surrounded the raids as well, and perhaps fueled the club owners' indignation. In the late 1950s and early 1960s, before he became district attorney, Garrison was a frequent patron at some of the Bourbon Street clubs he now targeted. Bedecked in a white dinner coat, the six feet, six inch Garrison was conspicuous as he lumbered from Lucky Pierre's to O'Brien's to the Playboy Club. He distributed business cards to customers at the Mardi Gras Lounge and once asked madam Norma Wallace to refer clients to him. Even after taking office in May 1962 and beginning his vice investigations later that summer, Garrison continued to visit his favorite French Quarter haunts despite objections from his staff and from Aaron Kohn, the Metropolitan Crime Commission's executive director. They argued Garrison should not deceive the public and crusade by day, while carousing by night. The district attorney dismissed those who called him a hypocrite and denied he wanted a reputation as a moralist. "It's not that I am against stripping," Garrison laughed to a *Washington Post* reporter in February 1963. He added, "I'm not a crusader. I'm just out to do my job and enforce the law. It just happens that B-drinking and prostitution are against the law." Such admissions only intensified the howls of those who felt the hypocritical Garrison had exceeded his authority.[8]

Soon, other law enforcement officials, notably the parish's criminal court judges and the city's police superintendent, added to the chorus of discontent concerning Garrison's raids. Louisiana law delegated investigative powers in New Orleans to the police force, not the District Attorney's Office. Although New Orleans police assigned a dozen investigators to the prosecutor's office, these officers historically had assisted solely in trial preparation. Since August, however, Garrison had used the investigators in his vice raids, over the objections of Police Superintendent Joseph I. Giarusso. "Let's not forget that he is the district attorney and I am the superintendent of police," Giarusso exhorted during a press conference when the feud between himself and Garrison became public, insisting, "Don't forget that distinction." Stung by Giarusso's scolding tone, Garrison alleged that police officers in New Orleans' First District, which included Bourbon Street and the entire French Quarter, displayed a "monumental disinterest" in ending vice conditions. Had these police officers cracked down on illegal activities, Garrison insisted, his office would not have needed to stymie prostitution, B-drinking, and other forms of vice. Giarusso challenged Garrison to produce evidence of malfeasance among the First District's officers; no charges resulted, but the district attorney's verbal barrage did not cease. In an August 30 statement to reporters, the prosecutor characterized Giarusso's stance toward his investigations as "curiously indistinguishable" from the attitudes of French Quarter vice operators and club owners. "They too feel that the district attorney has too many investigators, that the First District should remain dormant, and that the district attorney's cleanup of the Quarter should cease," Garrison asserted in a statement that foreshadowed his later accusations of racketeer influences against the judges.[9]

It was neither Giarusso nor vice operators who posed the most-serious threat to Garrison's investigations, however. In late August, the parish's eight criminal court judges, who controlled the district attorney's expenditures, began to question Garrison's extraordinary use of powers delegated to the city's police force. Like Giarusso, the judges maintained the district attorney had established "a second constabulary," acting not as a prosecutor, but as a police officer. Garrison responded to the charge with characteristic humor and egotism. "I have set up a 'second constabulary' because, so far as effective action on B-drink and vice goes, there is no *first* constabulary," he remarked to a reporter. A fundamental difference separated Garrison's feud with the judges and his row with the police department. The judges controlled the district attorney's finances. The Louisiana Legislature enacted a statute in 1950 that allowed the Orleans Parish district attorney to use funds collected from bond forfeitures and criminal case fines "at his discretion." In an apparent contradiction, however, the law also mandated that a district judge approve all expenditures from the fund.[10]

The fines and fees fund contained $1,700 when Garrison took office in May 1962. The account grew to $40,000 in about two months, largely because of the district attorney's crackdown on unpaid bond forfeitures. About a month into his tenure, Garrison began redecorating his offices, located at the southeast end of the block-long Criminal Courthouse at the intersection of Tulane and Broad avenues, covering the existing pink walls and exposed green pipes with richly colored walnut paneling. The judges approved $18,000 for Garrison to refurbish his office and to pay operational costs. After two months in office, Garrison spent nearly $2,500 for new office furniture, including $233 for plastic plants, $676 for a chartreuse carpet, and $309 for draperies. Another $14,000 in furnishings and other supplies remained unpaid when three judges informed Garrison on August 20 they would withhold further payments until the other five judges returned from their summer vacations. In a letter to the district attorney, the judges said they questioned the legality of the forfeiture statute and believed that they, in consultation with Garrison, could implement a better system. Garrison agreed the system needed an overhaul and secured a $5,000 personal loan from the Bank of New Orleans to pay some of the outstanding bills for office furniture, carpets, and faux shrubbery. In the days that followed, Garrison was not critical of the judges in any of his statements regarding the new financial limits placed on his office, and he never mentioned the effect the restraints would have on ongoing vice investigations. In fact, it was within days of the judges' decision that Garrison accused the city's police force, not the jurists, of "monumental disinterest" in vice prosecutions.[11]

Bourbon Street raids continued throughout September with no complaints—financial or otherwise—from the district attorney. When the judges returned from their vacations in early October, they met with Garrison to discuss the fines and fees system. Three issues precipitated their decision to restrict Garrison's funds, the judges told the district attorney. First, regulation of vice conditions was the jurisdiction of the police department, not the district attorney. Second, the fines and forfeitures statute, which gave the district attorney the right to use money in the account "at his discretion" while imposing judicial oversight of expenditures, appeared contradictory to the judges. Finally, the jurists had discovered that Garrison had gone from one judge to the next seeking approval for expenditures; if one judge declined, he went to another until he received authorization. The judges told Garrison he now would have to obtain the approval of five of the eight judges for expenditures from the account. Later, the judges made a significant addition to the new guidelines—they would no longer approve expenditures for vice investigations. Garrison issued no public statements about the restrictions, but he privately fumed over what he deemed the judges' attempt to control his office, and, in the next few weeks, it was apparent the judges intended to adhere to the new guidelines. On October 21, Garrison asked the judges for reimbursement of nearly $1,400 for expenses incurred by undercover vice investigators, but they refused. Five days later, the jurists approved more than $10,000 for some eighty properly documented bills for office expenses. Garrison could apply none of that amount to the $5,000 personal loan he had secured for the vice operations, however, and it appeared increasingly likely the district attorney would have to repay the loan himself. "There is a conspiracy among the judges to wreck my administration," Garrison told staff members during an October meeting.[12]

On October 26, the same day the judges approved $10,000 in funds for Garrison's office, the *Times-Picayune* published portions of a letter from Criminal Sheriff Louis A. Heyd Sr. to the criminal court judges. The parish prison, the sheriff wrote, had exceeded its capacity by 42 percent, and he asked the judges for suggestions to remedy the problem. District Attorney Garrison, the story noted, had offered to aid the sheriff in easing the prison overcrowding. In an October 31 letter to Senior Judge George Platt, Garrison suggested all criminal court sections begin holding court on Fridays, a day when many were not in session. He also suggested more jury trials in December and a temporary reduction in the judges' two-month summer vacations until the prison overcrowding problem lessened. The private letter was respectful and proactive; Garrison did not specifically name any judge and offered to change some of his office's operations in exchange for the jurists' cooperation in easing the jail overcrowding.[13]

Unaccountably, enmity saturated the public comments Garrison made the same day he delivered his courteous letter to Judge Platt. During a luncheon speech to the Temple Sinai Brotherhood, Garrison criticized the judges on a range of subjects and targeted, in particular, the number of vacations the jurists took annually. The judges received two and a half months of summer vacation in accordance with a Louisiana law enacted in the 1920s to free courts from holding sessions without the comfort of air conditioning. The law remained in effect into the 1960s, despite the installation of air conditioning in the courthouse the previous decade. In his speech, Garrison estimated the judges enjoyed more than two hundred days off the bench a year, not counting "All Saints' Day, Long's birthday, Memorial Day, and 'St. Winterbottom's Day.'" One judge, J. Bernard Cocke, refused to try cases on Fridays, but, Garrison quipped, Cocke "only takes Friday off once a week." Because of the judges' affinity for vacations, the parish prison had surpassed its capacity, Garrison claimed, repeating portions of Sheriff Heyd's letter in the *Times-Picayune* the previous week. Garrison said the only way to halt the judges' excessive vacations was "to publicize this racket of holidays." Later in the speech, he suggested the jurists believed their twelve-year terms made them impervious to criticism and compared them to "the sacred cows of India."[14]

It is not clear why Garrison chose his Temple Sinai speech to criticize the judges publicly for the first time. The prosecutor and the judges had held their previous negotiations regarding the distribution of funds in the fines and forfeitures account behind the fortress-like walls of the parish courthouse. He had agreed with the judges that the system needed an overhaul, and, only five days before, the judges had approved $10,000 in funds for his office. His letter to Judge Platt, written prior to the luncheon speech, was respectful and suggested a willingness to cooperate with the judges to lessen prison overcrowding. More notable, in neither the letter nor his speech did Garrison mention any judicial obstruction of his vice investigations, nor did he suggest a sinister motive behind the financial limits the jurists had placed on his office. Later, Garrison remarked that the judges' attempts to control his office necessitated his comments. "All I want to do is run my own office," he said after his defamation conviction in early 1963, insisting, "If I can't run it my way, I don't want it." At the time of Garrison's Temple Sinai remarks, however, the criticism seemed unexpected and perhaps unwarranted.[15]

New Orleans television stations reported the district attorney's luncheon remarks during their evening newscasts, and the city's two daily newspapers carried extensive coverage of his statements. The judges, in response, gathered on November 2 to discuss Garrison's accusations. Garrison quickly pointed out to reporters that the judges had scheduled their meeting on a Friday. "To my knowledge, this is the first time in the history of Criminal District Court that all the judges have come down to work on Friday," he said sarcastically, adding, "It makes me feel like I accomplished something." Queried by a reporter, Judge Shirley Wimberly called Garrison's accusations "wild" and attributed the district attorney's verbal barrage to the jurists' refusal to approve expenditures for rugs and drapes to redecorate Garrison's office. "The judges won't allow him to throw money around with both hands, like he was doing when he first became district attorney," Wimberly proclaimed. Garrison's allegations also elicited a rebuttal from recently retired Judge William O'Hara, who blamed the "outmoded" operations of Garrison's office for the backlog of cases awaiting trial. "Any lag in the disposition of cases is a direct result of inadequate operational methods of the district attorney's office about which the judges can do nothing and the district attorney can do everything," O'Hara insisted in a statement to the city's newspapers.[16]

The judges gathered the morning that Wimberly and O'Hara's statements appeared in the *Times-Picayune*. When Garrison arrived at his office that day, reporters from the *Picayune* and the *States-Item*, New Orleans' afternoon newspaper, asked the district attorney for a response to O'Hara's comments. The reporters' questions allowed Garrison to unload the resentment he had harbored against the judges since they first imposed monetary restrictions on his office in early October. Garrison first told the reporters that the fault for the overcrowded prisons and the exploding docket lay outside his office's purview. "District attorneys come and go every four years but the judges and the backlog always seem to be there," Garrison maintained. The district attorney then shifted his focus from the prison overcrowding to his vice investigations, "an operation with which the judges have shown a remarkable lack of sympathy," he charged. It was the first time Garrison publicly linked accusations of prison overcrowding with his vice crusade.[17]

In both the letter he wrote to Judge Platt on October 31 and in his Temple Sinai speech delivered that same day, Garrison never mentioned the anti-vice operations. Now, with attentive reporters scribbling furiously to keep up, the fast-talking district attorney's frustrations about the funding restrictions and the jail overcrowding merged into one blistering—and deceptive—attack. Although raids had continued throughout October and November, Garrison charged the judges had "completely blocked" his efforts. Without mentioning the judges' concerns of his use of police authority or the constitutionality of the fines and forfeitures statute, he said the jurists had tied "the purse strings of the district attorney's fines and fees" and had informed him that they would no longer approve expenditures for vice raids. In the remainder of his statement, Garrison clearly portrayed himself as a heroic figure, putting principle above punishment in his desire to do good. The district attorney continued:

> The judges have specifically directed that the district attorney's office "should not investigate anything" and informed me that they would allow me to use no further money from my large fines and fees—presently $40,000—for any form of vice investigation.

> In certain areas where we have spent borrowed money to keep operating against vice . . . the judges have instructed me that this money will not be replaced out of fines and fees. I must pay this money out of my own pocket.

Again, the message from the judges is clear. They do
not want the district attorney's office to investigate anything.

The judges have made it eloquently clear where their
sympathies lie in regard to aggressive vice investigations
by refusing to authorize use of the DA's funds . . . .

Again, the message is clear: "Don't rock the boat, son.
You are not supposed to investigate anything."

This raises interesting questions about racketeer influences on our eight vacation-minded judges.[18]

Garrison soon concluded his remarks, but the feud with the judges
was far from finished. His statements that day would transform what
had been a quarrel between stubborn jurists and an upstart district attorney into a watershed case that raised fundamental questions about
the place of public criticism in a democracy.

The district attorney's November 2 press statement represented
the intersection of the three undercurrents of *Garrison v. Louisiana*—
money, animosity, and deception. Throughout the early days of his
tenure as Orleans Parish's top prosecutor, Garrison never displayed
a penchant for subordination—his ego simply would not allow him
to appear inferior. To Garrison, money equaled power. Therefore, if
the judges controlled the district attorney's coffers, they effectively
controlled him. By cracking down on unpaid bond forfeitures after
he took office, Garrison increased the fines and fees fund to about
$40,000. He now believed it was his right to spend it as he wished.
As it appeared more likely he would have to repay the personal loan
he took out to fund his office "out of my own pocket," Garrison's animosity toward the judges grew and out of that animosity radiated the
deceptive nature of his allegations against them. In none of their written statements to the prosecutor did the judges tell him not to "investigate anything." Nor had the judges asked the district attorney to
avoid raiding clubs belonging to friends or known racketeers. They
simply asked him to refrain from spending additional funds from the
account until they could investigate the statute's legality. To Garrison,
the judges' actions signaled a death knell for his raids—and the favor-

able headlines the vice crackdown had garnered for him. To counter the stoppage, and to elevate himself to a heroic posture, Garrison then resurrected an accusation similar to the one he had made in August against Police Superintendent Giarusso and the city's police force. As in his earlier statement, the district attorney labelled any opposition to his actions as sympathy for vice operators. His plan, regardless of its deceitful nature, worked. Garrison's thousand-word statement, which would later form the basis of the state defamation prosecution against him, appeared verbatim in the *States-Item* on the afternoon of November 2.[19]

Garrison refused to meet later that day with the judges, who concluded their meeting with a joint press statement that castigated the prosecutor for his "intemperate" remarks in his Temple Sinai speech. The judges' comments again claimed the district attorney was deceptive in blaming others for the prison overcrowding. The district attorney, not the judges, controlled the docket, they said. The judges, probably unaware that Garrison's latest verbal barrage had appeared in the *States-Item* while they met, did not mention the allegation of "racketeer influences," but they requested that three state and local bar associations conduct ethics inquiries into Garrison's accusations. Bill Reed, news director at television station WWL, covered the judges' statement and then asked the district attorney to comment. "To be charitable," Garrison told Reed, "I would call that a lie," referring to the judges' contention that the district attorney controlled the docket. Reed asked Garrison why he refused to meet with the judges that day. "They know, I believe, perfectly well it would have been a waste of time," Garrison replied, continuing, "The only way to get these sacred cows back to work is by public reaction." The district attorney was far from finished. He continued to needle the judges mercilessly in the coming days, and the rift between him and the "sacred cows" only widened.[20]

Charges and countercharges continued throughout the next week. Garrison, in response to the judges' call for an ethics investigation, noted that the judges had demanded an inquiry into his allegations but not into overcrowding at the parish prison. He requested an independent probe of their "real motives for blocking and ending our investigation of B-drinking and other vice in New Orleans," a thinly veiled repetition of his earlier charge of racketeer influences. The *Times-Picayune* on November 4 carried a list of seventeen people Garrison alleged had awaited trial for more than a year while one judge, whom the district attorney declined to name, had not held court in six months. The following day's paper published a lengthy response from Judge Cocke, who admitted he was the unnamed judge and characterized Garrison's criticism as "unfounded and malicious." Cocke conceded Garrison was correct. He rarely held court on Fridays, but maintained he did so to allow assistant district attorneys a day to prepare the upcoming week's cases. However, the judge did not respond to Garrison's charge of his six-month hiatus from the bench, proclaiming instead, "I have never declined any request of any district attorney to hold court on a Friday if there were a need." In a letter responding to Cocke's statement, Garrison informed the jurist—whose acrimony toward the district attorney was matched only by Garrison's animus toward him—that he would schedule trial dates on Fridays beginning immediately, but when Garrison's assistant district attorney presented the docket files for that Friday's cases to Cocke's clerk, the clerk refused to accept them.[21]

Garrison attended a joint meeting of the judges on November 7. Two of the jurists, Brahney and Cocke, refused to attend when they learned the district attorney would be present. Leaving the meeting, Garrison uncharacteristically declined to answer reporters' questions. In a letter to Garrison that they later released to the press, the judges again denied the charges of judicial obstruction of vice investigations and said Garrison's attempts to "deliberately confuse and to give the general populace of New Orleans a contrary impression is certainly not in keeping with the high office you hold." There is no record of Garrison's reply, but the following day, November 8, the judges charged the district attorney with criminal defamation. Less than four hours after the judges filed the charges, Frank J. Klein, Garrison's first assistant, formally dismissed the accusations. Judge Platt signed the dismissal, perhaps indicating that he and his fellow jurists believed the charges had made their point. When Garrison refused to apologize publicly, however, the judges traveled as a group to Baton Rouge and asked Louisiana Attorney General Jack P.F. Gremillion to supersede Garrison and to reinstate the charges. Gremillion restored

the defamation case against Garrison on November 13 and said he
believed the district attorney's allegations had jeopardized "the integrity of our judicial system."[22]

Louisiana law at the time defined defamation as:

> The malicious publication or expression in any manner,
> to anyone other than the party defamed, or anything
> which tends: (1) To expose any person to hatred, con-
> tempt, or ridicule, or to deprive him of the benefit of pub-
> lic confidence or social intercourse; or (2) To expose the
> memory of one deceased to hatred, contempt, or ridicule;
> or (3) To injure any person, corporation, or association of
> persons in his or their business or occupation.[23]

If convicted, Garrison faced a maximum fine of three thousand dollars, one year in prison, or both, but these consequences did little to
dissuade the district attorney from continuing to criticize the judges.
Shortly after they charged him with defamation, Garrison issued an
indignant statement that maintained the judges' refusal to allocate
funds for his vice investigations compelled his public remarks. He
called the charges a "sideshow" and insisted, "if the . . . judges have
been injured, it is by their own conduct. They will have to do more
than this to stop me from telling the people the truth about the . . .
it will take more than this to block my office from investigating the
rackets." True to his word, and to demonstrate his refusal to allow
the judges to control his office, Garrison's anti-vice raids continued
throughout the remainder of 1962 and well into the following year.[24]

Garrison generally ignored the advice of his lawyers and assistant
district attorneys to remain silent prior to his trial. They believed the
judges and district attorney could reach an accord without the prosecution proceeding. Several public statements Garrison made before
his trial began in January only weakened the already fragile relationship between the prosecutor and the judges. For example, in early December, Garrison told an audience at St. Anthony Catholic Church
in New Orleans that the judges' refusal to allocate funds for his office
had halted his investigation completely. Here, as he would in numerous statements preceding his trial, Garrison failed to mention that his
investigators continued to infiltrate nightclubs along Bourbon and
Canal streets. Only the week before the St. Anthony speech, under-

cover work by investigators Malcolm Dodge, Theodore de la Houssaye, and Warren Moity had resulted in charges against five clubs for
B-drinking and prostitution. All five businesses eventually closed, although the judges refused to pay nearly $2,400 in expenses Garrison's
investigators claimed they had incurred.[25]

Speeches were not Garrison's only means of retribution against
the judges. He also initiated two separate court proceedings against
his chief nemesis, Judge J. Bernard Cocke. In early January 1963, a
week before Garrison's defamation trial began, an Orleans Parish
grand jury indicted Cocke for contempt, alleging the judge broke
grand jury secrecy rules during the questioning of a witness in an un-
related trial. After Garrison's defamation conviction, the grand jury
again indicted Cocke, this time for malfeasance for his refusal to approve $2,400 in expenditures for the district attorney's vice investiga-
tions. Garrison did not charge any of the other seven judges who also
had refused to allocate the funds. Few, including Garrison's assistant
district attorneys, doubted his motivations for prosecuting Cocke
were anything but political; he and the judge were bitter enemies long
before the current maelstrom. Early in Garrison's term, Cocke had
shouted at a meeting of the state Pardon Board that he considered
Garrison "persona non grata." Garrison claimed the judge's acrimony
resulted from his refusal to allow Cocke to have "control over the DA's
office," as past prosecutors had.[26]

The charges against Cocke were blatantly punitive. Garrison,
who acted as an adviser to the jury that indicted the judge, said the
$2,400 were expenses incurred by Warren Moity, Theodore de la
Houssaye, and Malcolm Dodge during undercover operations that
resulted in the closing of five Bourbon Street clubs.[27] In a letter saturated with spite, Garrison asked state Attorney General Gremillion to
prosecute Cocke on the malfeasance charges because "the integrity
of the judiciary may be involved"—the same reason Gremillion had
given reporters about his decision to prosecute Garrison. Gremillion
declined to supersede Garrison, and the district attorney prosecuted the cases himself when his assistants refused to participate in the
transparently retaliatory prosecution. Cocke won acquittal on both
the contempt and the malfeasance charges, but the losses did not
bother Garrison, former Assistant District Attorney Milton Brener

noted. "The humiliation to [Cocke] of being forced to sit at the bar as a common criminal was apparently sufficient," Brener suggested. The district attorney later targeted the twenty-year judicial veteran for defeat in the next election, and personally wrote campaign advertisements for Cocke's opponent, Assistant District Attorney Rudolph Becker. Becker won and became the second Criminal District Court judge to win election based largely on Garrison's support. New Orleans voters had elected the first, Frank Shea, to replace Judge Shirley Wimberly, who died in August 1963. Shea, Garrison's executive assistant, faced ten other candidates and had little popular support beyond some close friends and, of course, the district attorney. Shea narrowly defeated his opponent in a runoff, but Garrison's political strength had survived its first major electoral test. Garrison had proven his political acumen in citywide elections, and the remaining criminal court judges, realizing Garrison's popular appeal, began to work more favorably with the district attorney.[28]

Yet this eventual détente was not apparent as a new year dawned. Since late October 1962, Garrison had successfully shielded from the public the real underpinnings of his feud with the criminal bench. The ferocity with which Garrison lambasted the judges in statement after statement obscured the money, animosity, and deception that were at the heart of the brawl, and the district attorney did not intend to stop the barrage. Indeed, Garrison's fight with the jurists had tested his ability to navigate political minefields and to emerge unscathed. The campaign of ridicule he had launched against the judges was so successful that his political power had grown in the process, and Garrison would not stop publicly castigating his enemies even as his defamation trial began on January 21, 1963.

CHAPTER II

Judging the Judges:
A Trial—But for Whom?

On the night before Jim Garrison was to testify in his defamation trial, the Orleans Parish district attorney sat in his office, surrounded by aides. Garrison told them he had decided not to take the stand. In fact, he had instructed his attorneys to call none of the nearly two dozen witnesses they had summoned to appear in his defense. Assistant District Attorney Milton Brener, a witness to the scene, later recalled Garrison's "vivid description of his enemies sitting patiently for three days, salivating . . . over the prospect of his denouement on the stand." Garrison's argument for not mounting a defense, Brener asserted, was "that he had nothing to gain and everything to lose in the eyes of the public—the only court that concerned Jim Garrison." Garrison had little to fear. In the war of public perception, it was apparent he was already the victor.[1]

Since the beginning of the district attorney's trial on January 21, 1963, the city's daily newspapers featured prominent headlines proclaiming the salacious details that had emerged in court. One judge admitted he was the honoree at a party given by a known gambler. Another testified his late mother once owned a lottery operation. Yet another jurist stated that he regularly—and sometimes blindly—issued paroles for vice violators. As the hearing moved into its fourth day, and Garrison's attorneys prepared to call their own witnesses, it was increasingly unclear who was on trial—the district attorney or the eight judges. A former aide later recalled that Garrison believed "everyone reads the headlines concerning arrests and charges but few people read denials or correcting statements."[2]

If Garrison testified, he risked becoming the subject of those embarrassing headlines, and, as Brener asserted, the district attorney would rather lose the trial than damage his public image. There were sure to be questions about his own Bourbon Street escapades, about with whom he had cavorted in the past, about the clubs he had frequented, and about his relationships with some of the owners. For the first time publicly, Garrison would have to answer why he never expressed his concerns about overcrowding in the parish prison and about the judges' vacation schedules before making his scornful statements to the Temple Sinai Brotherhood luncheon on October 31, 1962. Furthermore, if the district attorney had evidence of racketeer influences on the judges, why did he not take a case to a grand jury instead of essentially indicting the jurists during a press conference on November 2? When Garrison refused to mount a defense, however, he spared himself those questions and succeeded in transforming his own trial into a referendum on the judges' fitness to hold office. This stratagem allowed Garrison to demonstrate to the judges that his political acumen included the ability to cull facts from their pasts that would embarrass them. It also permitted the district attorney to solidify his public image as an independent, reform-minded prosecutor who not only battled pimps and prostitutes but also the machine system that had dominated New Orleans politics for decades. For Garrison, ever eager to wrest control of power from the New Orleans establishment, this demonstration of political prowess and independence was a better outcome than the trial victory that eventually eluded him.[3]

In the month prior to his trial, Garrison continued to criticize the judges publicly while attempting to have the defamation charges dismissed. On November 16, 1962, three days after state Attorney General Jack P.F. Gremillion reinstated the charges against the prosecutor, Garrison attempted to file a motion to conduct an open hearing in the case instead of a trial. The prosecutor visited six courts before finding a judge who was working that Friday, something he delighted in pointing out to the press. "The judges say I am master of the dockets," Garrison said, referring to the schism between the jurists and the district attorney as to who was to blame for prison overcrowding, "but I am having a hard time finding just one of them on a Friday afternoon." Garrison told reporters he believed an open hearing would allow him more latitude in describing his side of the feud, but he and his attorneys later dropped the motion and asked instead for a jury trial. The Louisiana Constitution of 1921 did not require juries to decide misdemeanor offenses such as defamation, however. Garrison, perhaps believing New Orleans' citizens would sympathize with the plight of their crusading district attorney, asked for a jury and maintained state law violated the Sixth Amendment of the U.S. Constitution, which guaranteed jury trials and due process of law. Garrison's attorneys, Donald V. Organ and Louis P. Trent, also asked Judge William Ponder of Many, Louisiana, to recuse himself. The Louisiana Supreme Court had appointed Ponder to hear the case because all eight Orleans Parish judges were plaintiffs. In papers filed with the Criminal District Court, Organ said the defense sought Ponder's recusal based on Gremillion's November 13 statement in which he said, "the integrity of our judicial system is involved" in Garrison's case. By saying this, Gremillion had made all Louisiana judges plaintiffs in the case, Organ maintained. Additional pretrial motions asked that the court quash the charges against Garrison and demanded that the state highlight the specific defamatory passages in the district attorney's November 2 statement. Ponder denied all the motions and scheduled the trial to begin on January 21, 1963.[4]

As his attorneys planned their defense, Garrison continued to ridicule the judges publicly. He characterized the judges as "totalitarian" during a speech to a political association in mid-November, and implied the jurists were "using the machinery of the criminal district courts to counterattack me. Have they forgotten the First Amendment?" he asked, insisting, "I only exercised my right of free speech." In a December 5 address at St. Anthony's Catholic Church, Garrison repeated similar themes, comparing his prosecution to tactics employed in the Soviet Union to suppress dissent. He encouraged the audience to engage in vigorous criticism of public officials and assured them he would not charge them with defamation if they chose to be critical of him. As the speech reached its crescendo, the district attorney defended his accusations against the judges as "true . . . I will be standing up and telling the people of New Orleans every time I encounter trouble like this from a public official. I have to because I have no organization to turn to. I have no allies because the other officials are the association of armed robbers." A week prior to the beginning of his trial, an unrepentant Garrison told another civic group, "I have no apology for telling the people of New Orleans the truth," and continued, "I don't know if I would put it into greatly different words if I were to make these same complaints tomorrow." These final comments were not without provocation, however. Two days before, the judges told Garrison he would have to gain approval for all withdrawals from the fines and forfeitures account in advance, regardless of what the money was for. Furthermore, the judges instructed Garrison that they would not reimburse his staff members for expenses without prior approval. Garrison's inability to quell his public resentment toward the judges formed the nucleus of the prosecution's contention that he intended to malign the jurists' reputations.[5]

On January 21, the seething feud between Garrison and the judges moved into Section C of the Orleans Parish Criminal District Court. Over the next four days, the judges subjected themselves to embarrassing and discomforting testimony in order to prove that Garrison's accusations had exposed them to public ridicule. In addition, the judges unwittingly allowed the district attorney to use the court proceedings as a means to continue his public derision toward them and to portray himself as an alternative to New Orleans' political machine. Judge Ponder, from his vantage point on the bench, overlooked a strange scene as the trial began. Garrison, normally a habitué of the prosecution table, talked with his attorneys at the desk reserved for defendants. The parish's eight criminal judges, who would all testify, chatted among themselves while seated in the audience. If Ponder felt his surroundings odd, he perhaps found the testimony that surfaced during the trial equally as strange—judges cavorting with known gamblers, issuing countless paroles for vice operators, and enforcing some laws while pleading ignorance of others. It was Garrison's trial in name only. The real defendants were the eight judges whose fitness for office was under scrutiny.[6]

Testimony from New Orleans print and television reporters who covered Garrison's numerous statements concerning the judges consumed the majority of the trial's first day, although the judges' testimony comprised most of the four-day proceeding. Judge Malcolm V. O'Hara, the newest member of the criminal bench, was the first judge to take the stand. He and Garrison were assistant district attorneys together in the mid-1950s, and when O'Hara unsuccessfully sought the top prosecutor's spot in the 1958 election, he had promised to make Garrison his first assistant. O'Hara became a judge in September 1962, in the early stages of the growing rift between the criminal court and the district attorney. His testimony was far less colorful—and less embarrassing—than the other judges' subsequent statements. In order to prove defamation, the state needed to establish that Garrison's accusations subjected them to "hatred, contempt, or ridicule." Attorney General Gremillion, who prosecuted the case, asked each judge if he had suffered public enmity after Garrison's remarks. O'Hara said he had experienced "some" ill will because of the district attorney's comments. "People jokingly ask me if it is true that we get all these vacations, whether or not I am a sacred cow, or whether I am influenced by racketeers," O'Hara testified. He added that he believed "the criminal bench seems to be getting the worst of public opinion" while the district attorney's public stature and political influence had risen. As the trial progressed, it became apparent that Garrison intended to use the proceedings to muddy further the judges' reputations and to bolster his standing both with the public and within the political realm.[7]

Testimony from O'Hara's father, retired Judge William O'Hara, followed, and the elder jurist's statements were far less restrained. Although William O'Hara was not among the eight judges who were plaintiffs in the case, he issued a statement to the press after Garrison's October 31, 1962, allegations that excessive judicial vacations had exploded the parish's criminal docket and had inundated the prison system. In the statement, O'Hara blamed outmoded operations in the District Attorney's Office for the case backlog. In turn, these comments provoked Garrison to issue his November 2 statement that charged "racketeer influences" on the parish's "eight vacation-minded judges." In his testimony, the judge admitted he harbored animosity toward the district attorney for not implementing office procedures similar to those utilized by former District Attorney Leon D. Hubert, under whom Garrison had served as an assistant district attorney in the mid-1950s. "Mr. Garrison can run his office any way he wants to, but he's got no business blaming his deficiencies on the courts," O'Hara asserted. O'Hara's testimony only supported Garrison's contention that his refusal to allow the judges to run his office led them to limit his finances. It also bolstered an image Garrison believed would win him the public's support—that of an independent prosecutor who represented an alternative to the establishment and its antiquated control of the city.[8]

The former judge denied that his animosity toward Garrison had resulted in his refusal to approve expenditures for the District Attorney's Office. O'Hara admitted he had declined to sign a $985 expenditure for carpets and drapes for Garrison's private office and characterized the cost as "extravagant." The judge recalled that he had told Garrison to ask for bids from other firms to verify the district attorney had received the best price, but that Garrison had not returned with the additional paperwork. Defense attorney Organ targeted O'Hara's ignorance of state law, which did not require competing bids for items less than $1,000. The revelation that he had not followed a key statute and, in fact, had approved thousands of dollars for previous district attorneys without adhering to the state's bid law, embarrassed the former judge. Organ continued to inundate O'Hara with questions about expenditures the judge had authorized for past district attorneys. Organ presented the former judge with two bills he signed for then-District Attorney Richard Dowling that authorized the prosecutor to purchase a 1960 Pontiac for $3,385 and a 1961 Cadillac for $6,122. Organ asserted that O'Hara allowed Dowling to purchase both automobiles "without bids or without advertisement" in violation of "the letter of the law." O'Hara, obviously discomforted by the suggestion that he was ignorant of state law, replied that he had been unhappy with the system of approving expenditures even before Garrison took office and had allowed Dowling to purchase the automobiles although he "didn't like it a bit." Although this questioning certainly did not reveal any racketeer influences on the elder O'Hara, Organ nonetheless raised the specter that the judges had held previous district attorneys to a different standard than they had Garrison—again underlining Garrison's contention that his independence threatened the judges' fierce partisanship and instigated the defamation charges he now faced.[9]

Organ similarly questioned the next witness, Judge Shirley G. Wimberly, and attempted to prove the judge had held Garrison to a stricter financial standard than he had previous district attorneys. Wimberly, who claimed to have received "many telephone calls of derision" as a result of Garrison's accusations, testified that he had approved expenditure vouchers because Garrison had claimed Judge William O'Hara had agreed previously to sign them but had failed to do so before he left on vacation. Wimberly said he later discovered Garrison had misled him and this deception "was the reason for the judges deciding that they would require five judges to sign all subsequent motions." Wimberly further testified that the judges halted payments for Garrison's vice investigations because state law granted the police force, not the District Attorney's Office, sole responsibility for investigative work within the city limits. Organ highlighted incongruities within Wimberly's statements—how, he asked, could the judge strictly enforce state law governing police powers, but usurp the law dictating the required number of judicial signatures on expenditures for the District Attorney's Office? Futhermore, Organ asked, why had Wimberly approved more than $1,000 for previous prosecutors without question, but had required Garrison to take extraordinary measures to secure less funding? "Strange as it may seem," Wimberly snapped, "I don't know all the law on earth," a surprising admission from someone who had practiced law for four decades.[10]

Organ continued to allege that the judges required more of Garrison than they had of previous district attorneys. Organ produced several Wimberly-approved vouchers for extradition trips assistant district attorneys had taken during the term of Garrison's predecessor. One $65 item, labeled simply "Recreation," received Wimberly's approval, and the judge admitted he had not asked the assistant district attorney for any explanation as to how he spent the money. "Well, rather than sit in a hotel room all evening," Wimberly theorized, "I would think they might be entitled to go to a picture show or something like that." Organ queried: "Sixty-five dollars worth of picture show?" "Over a period of days, yes, or a Broadway show maybe," Wimberly responded, adding, "Those things cost money." Stubbornly, the judge refused to concede that he had applied a different standard to Garrison's expenditures than he had with previous prosecutors. Wimberly did not have to, however, and by putting another of Garrison's accusers on the defensive, Organ again succeeded in reinforcing Garrison's independence of the inveterate politicians who now stood as his accusers.[11]

As his testimony continued, Wimberly attempted to ridicule Garrison for requesting funds to redecorate his office, but Organ quickly put the judge back on the defensive with questions about the number of paroles he had granted for prostitutes, B-drinkers, and gamblers. Wimberly testified the judges had approved $233 for "two plastic plants. . . . That was a great necessity for the District Attorney's Office, wasn't it?" Furthermore, the judges allowed Garrison to spend nearly $300 on a couch and overstuffed chair. "You are really living in comfort over there, Brother," he addressed a nonplussed Garrison, "you are really living in comfort." Wimberly abandoned the air of levity when Organ began to question him about nearly 140 vice-related paroles the judge had granted over a twenty-two month period. Furthermore, Wimberly had granted almost 100 of those paroles within two hours of arrest, Organ asserted. Such prompt paroles allowed "these lottery operators and B-drinkers to be back in business on the same night" of their arrests, Organ insisted. Wimberly agreed: "Yes, and if you parole a man for disturbing the peace, that allows him to get out and disturb the peace again fifteen minutes after he is out if you are going to use that theory." Wimberly bristled at Organ's implication that he had issued paroles "for the purpose of letting [criminals] go back in business." The defense attorney denied making such allusions, but added that the rapid paroles were "in complete accord with what they would want on Bourbon Street." Embarrassed and angry, Wimberly countered that he did not issue paroles for Bourbon Street habitués, but rather for lawyers and friends who requested paroles for themselves, clients, or acquaintances. Although such questions had not proven racketeer influences on the judge, Wimberly left the stand with the image of shady deals and double standards surrounding his testimony. Garrison and his attorneys continued to infer similar nefarious connections during their questioning of subsequent witnesses.[12]

Judge Oliver Schulingkamp was the next witness, and like the other judges, stated he believed Garrison had assumed extra-prosecutorial duties when he had initiated his Bourbon Street cleanup. The judge insisted state law gave the police department the authority to "ferret out crime of all types," and that he and the other judges would not continue to approve funds for Garrison "to play Mr. District Attorney á la television." In subsequent questioning, however, Organ implied Schulingkamp had stopped funding Garrison's anti-vice operations because the jurist was under the sway of known racketeers.

The judge admitted being the guest of honor at a party given by Mike Callia, whom Organ characterized as a "gambler of long standing." Schulingkamp denied he knew how Callia earned a living, but said the party Callia hosted following the judge's inauguration in January 1960 was "unexpected, unsolicited, but nevertheless appreciated." Schulingkamp further admitted he had issued paroles for Rip Robert, a known lottery operator from whom the judge also had purchased clothes, and for Peter Hand, a former state legislator who had faced charges of extortion and gambling. The judge remained unapologetic for issuing paroles, even for known vice operators like Hand and Robert. "It sets at liberty a person who otherwise would have to remain in jail," he asserted, adding that paroles relieved "the crowded situation that Mr. Garrison talks about in the parish prison." Schulingkamp's dismissive answer only worked to Organ's advantage and again raised the possibility that Garrison's allegations contained an element of truth.[13]

Mike Callia emerged again in the testimony of Judge Edward A. Haggerty Jr., who followed Schulingkamp on the stand. As he had with Schulingkamp, Organ used Haggerty's association with a known gambler to embarrass the jurist and to imply that Garrison's accusation of "racketeer influences" had merit. As his testimony commenced, Haggerty asserted that Garrison's statements had "irreparably injured" his reputation. The jurist said that on at least a dozen occasions—in such respected places as Brennan's restaurant and the New Orleans Athletic Club—people "mooed" at him, a reference to Garrison's "sacred cows" allegation. "They make remarks that you are always on vacation," Haggerty complained under direct questioning from Attorney General Gremillion, "they make remarks that they didn't realize the judges didn't work . . . I feel that I myself have been immeasurably injured, embarrassed, and have been subjected to ridicule." Under cross-examination from Organ, however, Haggerty left the impression that his poor public reputation was the result of personal behavior, not Garrison's accusations. Haggerty admitted he, like Schulingkamp, attended parties given by Mike Callia and ate in a restaurant owned by Francis Giardina. As an assistant district attorney, Haggerty prosecuted both Callia and Giardina on vice charges, but now was unapologetic for continuing to socialize with them. "I paid my bill," Haggerty said of dining in Giardina's restaurant, adding, "If we had been that friendly, I think he would have put it on the house." Haggerty also admitted he paroled prisoners at the request of Mike Roach, who appeared in the judge's court on a prostitution charge. "I'm not trying to be a character witness for him," the judge insisted, but added that he would issue another parole for Roach if asked. Haggerty's obstinacy worked in Organ's favor. He demonstrated again an incontrovertible link between a member of the criminal bench and a known felon and had reinforced the idea that the judges' moral ineptitude made them unfit to control the funds of a prosecutor determined to eliminate vice in his city.[14]

With the image of a judge associating with felons again permeating the courtroom, Organ turned to another favorite element of his defense—the idea that the judges had applied the fines and forfeitures law to Garrison in a manner different than they had previous district attorneys. Haggerty garnered a laugh when he said he had signed fewer vouchers for Garrison than the other judges because his chambers were located "so far distant from the District Attorney's Office." Nevertheless, Organ presented Haggerty with an expense report he signed that approved more than $1,800 incurred by two assistant district attorneys during an extradition trip to New York City in 1960, two years before Garrison took office. The pair spent nearly $500 for meals over a five-day period. "Now, judge, would you have to say they were very liberal in food?" Organ asked Haggerty, who answered affirmatively but admitted he had approved the expense report without question.[15]

Organ spared judges Thomas M. Brahney Jr. and Bernard J. Bagert Sr. the discomforting questions to which he had subjected previous witnesses. Unable to cull embarrassing incidents from the pasts of the two reputable jurists, Organ instead asked them about the forfeiture law's constitutionality. During his testimony, Brahney asserted his belief that the entire feud over monetary appropriations between Garrison and the judges could have been settled in another forum without the row becoming public. Both Brahney and Bagert said they had continued to sign vouchers for the district attorney— sometimes over the objections of their fellow jurists—because no higher court had ruled on the forfeiture statute's viability. "It is my

opinion that the whole fines and fees statute is unconstitutional,"
Bagert said, continuing, "As long as the statute is in existence and has
not been ruled unconstitutional, if some reasonable explanation was
given . . . I would sign for a reasonable amount of money to be spent."
The rational and detached answers from the two jurists perhaps concerned Garrison's counsel. When Garrison had alleged criminal influence on "our eight vacation-minded judges," he had not allowed for
the possibility that he had not meant the entire bench. Now, Bagert
and Brahney's testimony revealed that two of the judges had continued to provide funds for his vice cleanup. Because Garrison had included all of the judges in his statement, it now appeared his remarks
had impugned the reputations of at least two of them. Fortunately for
Garrison's defense, subsequent witnesses' testimony all but cleansed
the notion from the courtroom that Garrison indeed had libeled the
two jurists. The statements of two other judges illustrated Garrison's
ability to cull events from his opponents' past that sullied their fitness
to hold office. By placing the judges on the defensive, again Garrison
maintained his image as a crusader attempting to shake the control of
entrenched, morally unfit politicians.[16]

If Garrison's attorney treated Bagert and Brahney gently, he
extended no such courtesy to Senior Judge George W. Platt. Under
cross-examination, Platt denied any affiliation with vice operators.
Organ then presented the judge with a 1946 contract, signed by Platt's
mother, which transferred ownership of the Original Claiborne Lottery from the Platt family to another man for $1,000. Platt backped-
aled and asserted his father, not his mother, had owned a lottery operation prior to his death in 1938 and that he could only assume it
was the same business his mother had later sold. Nevertheless, Organ
once again embarrassed one of Garrison's accusers. Although Platt's
testimony did not truly prove he was under racketeers' influence, it
did raise the possibility that truth colored Garrison's criticism of the
judges.[17]

By the time Judge J. Bernard Cocke took the stand, Organ had
elicited humiliating testimony from four of Cocke's fellow judges—
Wimberly, Schulingkamp, Haggerty, and Platt. Cocke attempted
early in his testimony to embarrass Garrison instead. The judge
condemned Garrison's chief investigator Pershing O. Gervais as "a

thief, a grafter . . . a habitué of the places in the French Quarter they now denounce." He described Frank J. Klein, first assistant district attorney, as "incompetent," and the judge became so belligerent that Organ requested that Judge Ponder ask the witness to put down his fist and to stop waving his finger. Such demonstrative behavior was expected—Garrison and Cocke were longtime foes. Cocke once accused Garrison of attempting to intimidate the state Parole Board and referred to the district attorney during a parole hearing as "persona non grata." Garrison brought charges of malfeasance against Cocke only a few weeks before the start of the defamation trial, but Organ did not mention the recent allegations against the judge. Instead, he resurrected allegations from a political campaign twenty years before during which the candidates had traded barbs similar to Garrison's accusations. During the 1942 race for district attorney, in which Cocke ran as the incumbent, opponent Cicero Sessions alleged Cocke "associated with gangsters and crooks and has no intention of abolishing organized vice in this city." Sessions further described Cocke as being "hand in hand," with a group of racketeers and city officials that was "in parallel in its viciousness and corruption to Murder, Incorporated." Sessions' charges against Cocke surpassed Garrison's later allegations in viciousness, and as Organ read them into the record, Cocke attempted several times to interrupt him. Sessions' accusations continued:

> That is why I call this man 'Judas-Brutus-Cockey,' because he is the biggest turncoat and political hypocrite ever to disgrace public office in the state of Louisiana. His position as a racket-controlled, racket-supported district attorney is by now so well known that the gracious thing for him to do would be to retire promptly to the private life which he abhors and which he found exceedingly uncomfortable during the time he was off the public payroll.[18]

Another opponent in the 1942 district attorney's race was Shirley Wimberly, another plaintiff in the defamation case against Garrison. During the race, Wimberly accused Cocke of exceeding his jurisdiction—the exact charge the judges now leveled against Garrison. Cocke conceded he believed both Sessions and Wimberly's statements had qualified as defamation, but he had not charged either man because he won re-election and "after having already whipped him, I didn't see any reason to be bothered any more about it, because the public didn't believe it." Organ replied, "My point is this, judge: You have never filed a criminal defamation charge against any one of these people before, and you have never filed a libel suit against the people who made these statements." Organ ignored the fact that Garrison had not issued his statements during the middle of an election, as had Sessions and Wimberly. Although the defense attorney's comparison between the two incidents was faulty, he nonetheless succeeded in resurrecting fierce opinions about Cocke that supported Garrison's more-recent accusations.[19]

The state ended its case after calling a final witness, Police Superintendent Joseph I. Giarusso, whose testimony concerned the dozen police officers the department assigned to the District Attorney's Office. Giarusso testified that the city of New Orleans paid the police officers. As a result, their salaries did not come from the fines and fees account, which allowed Garrison to continue using these officers in vice raids long after the district attorney claimed the judges had halted his investigations. With that final indictment of Garrison's honesty, Gremillion rested the state's case. Seconds later, Organ also rested. Whispers emanated throughout the courtroom. Many expected Garrison to testify on his own behalf, but the district attorney, realizing the damage such testimony could have on his public image, told his attorneys not to mount a defense. The list of defense witnesses reveals the testimony Garrison and his attorneys would have attempted to elicit, however. Nearly two dozen names comprised the list and included Andrew Monte, Frank Giardina, Mike Callia, and Alex Berger, all of whom Organ mentioned as he questioned the judges about their associations with known racketeers. The defense obviously intended to ask these disreputable witnesses to describe their relationships with the criminal court judges in an attempt to humiliate further the already-embarrassed jurists. The presence of their names on the witness list certainly could have been a calculated attempt on the part of Garrison's attorneys to encourage the judges to be as forthcoming as possible in their testimony. By having the judges damage their own reputations rather than eliciting testimony from criminals, Garrison maintained the independent image he so forcefully cultivated. He hoped that the public noticed that, unlike the jurists, he did not associate with criminals. Had the judges been less than forthright in their answers, however, Garrison undoubtedly would have used these witnesses in his defense.[20]

Closing arguments commenced ten days after both sides rested. Ponder delayed the summations so he could consider seventeen points of law Organ had presented him. These arguments detailed nuances of the state statutes governing defamation and examined federal and state court precedents. At the beginning of the prosecution's closing statements, Attorney General Gremillion noted that the defense "went out of its way" to continue to ridicule the judges, but that Organ "introduced no evidence whatsoever to contradict the findings that the malicious statement was made." Gremillion insisted that the state had shown that Garrison's accusations had subjected the judges to contempt, hatred, and ridicule—the parameters state law established to define defamation. "We have proved beyond a reasonable doubt that he went out of his way to attack these judges," the attorney general argued, adding, "We proved he called them 'sacred cows,' we proved he accused them of running rackets, we have proved . . . he went out of his way to defame," the judges. "Being merely a district attorney does not and never did give him the authority to be a character assassin," Gremillion concluded. The attorney general's final comment again implied that Garrison had impugned the judges' reputations intentionally. Gremillion's characterization of the district attorney as a "character assassin" went beyond any previous indictment of Garrison's moral certitude, however. Gremillion now implied that Garrison acted with the intentions of a killer—to use his remarks against the judges as a weapon to destroy their reputations and to assume their power as his own.[21]

In his closing statement, Organ attempted to remove the cloak of guilt from his client and to transfer it to the jurists by again asserting Garrison's independence from the old-time politicians who controlled New Orleans with little regard for ethics or the law. He reiterated the belief that the judges attempted to control Garrison's finances more closely than they had the expenditures of political cronies who had previously served as district attorney. Organ further suggested that the judges had ignored some laws, such as the state's bid statute, and had usurped others, such as the fines and forfeitures rule. Previous prosecutors' administrations experienced "an absolutely free hand on authorizing funds for the use of the District Attorney's Office, a free hand to the extent that they ignored the public bidding law, to the extent that men were allowed to charge for . . . entertainment . . . a free hand in that they were allowed to buy Cadillacs," Organ recalled. The judges had not required previous district attorneys to obtain competing bids for items over $1,000, as the law required, although they had insisted Garrison obtain alternate bids for expenses less than that sum, Organ argued. Furthermore, the defense attorney continued, the jurists had circumvented the fines and forfeitures statute by insisting Garrison win the approval of five of the judges for financial reimbursements, although the law required only one signature. As he concluded his statements, Organ elevated Garrison to the heroic posture the prosecutor so cherished. "Jim Garrison . . . is guilty of one thing and one thing only, and this is of running a good District Attorney's Office and being a good District Attorney," Organ insisted, adding, "If . . . Mr. Garrison is prevented from making public statements . . . then we think freedom of speech is walking a very dangerous and narrow path." With this final appeal, Organ again implied that the judges, not Garrison, broke the law, closing his summation with the image that the judges were morally and ethically unfit to control the funds of an independent, reform-minded district attorney.[22]

Judge Ponder issued his ruling on February 6, 1963. In a forty-page opinion, Ponder asserted that the district attorney's repeated attacks on the judges, often in the media's presence, demonstrated he had intended to defame them. He maintained that Garrison had based his statements not on truth, but on "provocation, ill-feeling, spite and enmity . . . over the judges' failure to approve his expenditures." Ponder stated that he could not conclude that Garrison "could have had a reasonable belief" that all eight judges were under racketeers' influence, and he dismissed the defense's assertion that the First Amendment protected the accusations. "Legitimate criticism of public officials should never be abridged," Ponder insisted, adding, "I cannot subscribe to the theory that all acts of public officials can be criticized with impunity." With that, Ponder found Garrison guilty and set sentencing for the last day of February.[23]

Throughout his trial, Garrison remained silent and uncharacteristically declined to answer reporters' questions outside the courtroom. During the proceedings, the district attorney focused on a yellow legal pad in front of him and appeared to be taking copious notes concerning the testimony. In actuality, Garrison, a frustrated playwright and novelist, was composing a satire based on Shakespeare's *Richard the Third*. Entitled *King James the First*, the play pits the hero—James— against a collection of ignoble dukes, based unapologetically on the judges, his accusers. With the trial over, however, Garrison no longer restrained himself. "As an American citizen, I have the right to criticize any public official who seems to be doing his duty improperly," Garrison insisted in a newspaper statement just hours after his conviction. The district attorney said he intended "to exercise my constitutional rights to speak freely" and would "continue to investigate organized crime without any letup." On February 28, 1963, Ponder fined Garrison $1,000 and ordered him jailed for four months if he did not pay it. The district attorney and defense team immediately filed an appeal with the Louisiana Supreme Court, which had original jurisdiction over cases involving district attorneys and members of the judiciary. Had Garrison paid the fine, the money would have gone into the fines and fees account that funded his office. Garrison privately joked he would commission a $1,000 portrait of himself to hang in his private office. His chief investigator, Pershing Gervais, suggested a frightening likeness of Judge J. Bernard Cocke, his chief antagonist, instead. Garrison liked the idea, but his assistants talked him out of it.[24]

It was unusual for anyone to talk Garrison out of anything. Indeed, the independent streak he fiercely cultivated—and hoped the public noticed—inspired his feud with the judges and underlined Garrison's quest to topple New Orleans' existing political establishment. The prosecutor's desired autonomy dictated the ferocity with which he attacked the judges' fitness to hold office and their control over his finances. Before his trial, Garrison criticized the judges repeatedly and alleged a litany of misdeeds, but the trial itself allowed his attorneys to elicit testimony from the judges that succeeded in embarrassing the jurists far greater than Garrison ever could. By the end of the fourth day of testimony, the trial became a referendum on the moral certitude of the Orleans Parish criminal bench and a clear demonstration of Garrison's political acumen and independence. The district attorney's influence only strengthened as his conviction moved through the appeals process. On the appellate level, however, the case moved beyond its original malevolence, as the attorneys infused the case with questions about the right to a jury trial and the nature of free speech. In the process, *Garrison v. Louisiana* shed its origins as a turf war that benefited one individual politically and began to reformulate as a case that enhanced First Amendment protections for all Americans.[25]

CHAPTER III

Supreme Stepping Stone:
A Landmark Takes Shape

Jim Garrison was certain that the U.S. Supreme Court was the only place he could get a fair hearing. In New Orleans, he had accumulated too many political and personal enemies—the police force, the judges, and the nightclub owners on Bourbon Street, to name a few. He further doubted the Louisiana Supreme Court's impartiality in his case. He characterized the court as a partisan body and his style of independent politics threatened the inveterate politicians who comprised the state's highest court. Yet the seven members of the Louisiana Supreme Court formed a barrier between the district attorney and the fairness he expected from the U.S. Supreme Court. In order to demonstrate his cause's rectitude to the highest court in the nation, Garrison and his attorneys needed to abandon the scandalous details and salacious testimony that had characterized the lower court prosecution. As the first step in the appellate process, the Louisiana Supreme Court served as a forum for the district attorney to transform his case from one based on political animosity into an appeal that raised questions about the First Amendment right of individuals to criticize their elected leaders without fear of retribution. Within the confines of the Louisiana Supreme Court, Garrison's case ceased to be a local, partisan squabble from which an individual emerged triumphant and instead became an appeal whose questions about the place of free speech in a constitutional democracy would benefit all Americans.

Garrison's appeal to the Louisiana Supreme Court contained more than two dozen bills of exception, official grievances with rulings trial Judge William Ponder had made during the lower court proceedings. As the case moved through the appellate process, the defense abandoned many of these complaints; arguments that raised the most significant constitutional questions, such as the right to a fair trial and the legality of the Louisiana defamation statute, remained however. The defense based its assertion that the state had denied Garrison a fair trial on two contentions. The first explored Judge Ponder's refusal

45

to recuse himself from the case. When he had reinstated the defamation charge against Garrison, state Attorney General Jack P.F. Gremillion remarked that "the integrity of the judiciary is involved" in the feud between Garrison and the jurists.[1] Gremillion's statement had made all of the state's judges interested parties in the case, the defense contended, and Ponder's refusal to recuse himself had violated the Sixth and Fourteenth Amendments' due process guarantees. "In the minds of the general public, this case became the case of the District Attorney versus the Judiciary," Garrison's attorney, Donald V. Organ, suggested in his brief, in which he concluded a verdict in Garrison's favor "would have condemned the judiciary, particularly in the eyes of the public." Therefore, Ponder could not render an impartial verdict because to do so essentially would have been a denunciation of himself. "The judiciary could not stand in a position of the accusers, the judge, the jury, and the executioners and give Jim Garrison a constitutional trial," Organ insisted.[2]

In retrospect, the initial argument on Ponder's fitness to hear Garrison's case seems a bit hackneyed, an example of legal wrangling based more on semantics than law. The Louisiana Supreme Court dismissed this claim, as it did each of the bills of exception, and the defense would not resurrect the stipulation in its later appeal to the U.S. Supreme Court. However, Garrison's attorneys continued to assert throughout the appellate process a second argument that attacked the legality of the lower court proceedings—that Louisiana law had violated Garrison's Sixth Amendment rights by denying him a trial by jury. Louisiana law stipulated that a jury was unnecessary in misdemeanor cases such as defamation. This was unacceptable, Organ insisted, because the "right to a trial by jury is essential to a fair trial." The defense then cited the U.S. Supreme Court case of *Gideon v. Wainwright*, which the court had decided on March 18, 1963, less than two months before. In *Gideon*, the court held that defendants in state cases were entitled to counsel and characterized this right as fundamental to democracy. In relation to Garrison's case, however, the *Gideon* citation seemed immaterial; *Gideon* had dealt not with trial by jury, but rather with the right of defendants to counsel. Organ cited *Gideon* merely to bolster his contention that the right to a jury trial "is even more fundamental and essential to a fair trial than is the right to counsel." In its eventual ruling, the Louisiana Supreme Court noted the irrelevancy of the *Gideon* citation, and Garrison's attorneys abandoned references to the case in subsequent filings with the U.S. Supreme Court.[3]

As his brief to the Louisiana Supreme Court continued, Organ intertwined the jury trial contention with an argument about freedom of speech that ultimately played a key role in the U.S. Supreme Court's decision. Free speech cases enhanced the importance of a jury trial, he insisted. Organ reasoned that the Constitution's framers had recalled the seditious libel trial of colonial printer John Peter Zenger when they had inserted a jury trial protection into the Bill of Rights. In his defense of Zenger, attorney Andrew Hamilton had argued that a jury of Zenger's peers, not a judge, should decide his fate. The judge had allowed a jury to consider the Zenger case, and it had acquitted the printer. "As the Englishmen and American colonists of the eighteenth century learned through bitter experience, a jury is absolutely essential in seditious libel trials to protect the constitutional rights of a person who . . . dares to criticize the actions of powerful officials," Organ concluded. The attorney's characterization of the Louisiana defamation statute as a sedition law—which governments historically had used to punish critics—was significant, and the defense continued to characterize the statute similarly as the case moved through the appellate process.[4]

Organ again described the state defamation law as a sedition statute as he shifted his brief's focus from the jury trial demand to its most significant contention—the suggestion that the Louisiana law violated the First Amendment's free speech guarantees. These assertions remained central to Garrison's appeal, not only at the state level, but before the nation's highest court as well. "Any law which in any fashion curtails freedom of expression violates the First Amendment to the Federal Constitution," Organ asserted. The 1921 Louisiana Constitution guaranteed no prior restraint, defined as government interference to block publication or, in the case of speech, expression. The defense argued, however, that the First Amendment to the U.S. Constitution surpassed mere restrictions on prior restraint. Organ quoted legal scholar Zechariah Chafee's *Free Speech in the United States* (1946) in which Chafee wrote, "The First Amendment was written by men . . . who intended to wipe out the common law of sedition, and make further prosecutions for criticism of the government forever impossible in the United States." Associate Supreme Court Justice Hugo Black and other First Amendment absolutists, who believed free speech should be totally uninhibited by law, shared Chafee's sentiment, Organ contended. "History shows that seditious libel is nothing more than the prosecution of people who are on the wrong side politically," he insisted, adding, "They have said something which antagonizes or threatens those who are in power." The attorney then compared the defamation statute to the federal Sedition Act of 1798, enacted to suppress anti-Federalist sentiment among newspapers during the administration of President John Adams. The U.S. Supreme Court never considered a challenge to the law, which expired at the end of Adams' term in 1801. Organ insisted that had the high court heard such a case, it invariably would have nullified the act as a violation of the First Amendment's free speech clause, as was the Louisiana defamation law. The Louisiana Supreme Court eventually dismissed the assertion, but the defense continued to characterize the defamation law as a sedition statute when it argued the appeal before the U.S. Supreme Court.[5]

Continuing his effort to prove Garrison's defamation conviction violated the First Amendment's free speech guarantees, which stood as the appeal's most significant constitutional argument, Organ cited the U.S. Supreme Court's decision in *Schenck v. U.S.* (1919), which in 1963 remained the legal standard for determining the criminality of words. In *Schenck*, the court had held that the First Amendment did not protect speech that constituted a "clear and present danger" to society. Yet Ponder had "brushed aside" the "clear and present danger" test in Garrison's case, essentially ignoring the legal yardstick the Supreme Court had established, Organ asserted. Had he applied the *Schenck* test, Ponder would have discovered "no substantive evil which justifies punishment of this accused," the attorney insisted. Based on this assertion, Organ once again characterized Garrison's conviction as unconstitutional.[6]

Futhermore, Organ suggested that as a public official speaking on a matter of public importance, Garrison enjoyed greater First Amendment protections. The doctrine of qualified privilege shielded officials' comments about public affairs or about other officials, he argued. Such an argument was not legally path breaking. In *Wood v. Georgia* (1962), the U.S. Supreme Court held that "the role public officials play in our society makes it all the more impressive that they be allowed freely to express themselves on matters of current public importance." Garrison did just that, Organ argued, and his actions did not constitute malice toward the judges. "There was an amazing attitude expressed by [Gremillion] and [Ponder] . . . that the accused should not have made his views about the judges' obstructionary tactics known to the public," he contended, asking rhetorically, "And this is democracy? How are the people to know what their elected officials are doing, if they cannot be told?" Organ concluded that Garrison's comments were privileged assertions made by a district attorney for the benefit of the citizens of New Orleans, and, under the court's ruling in *Wood v. Georgia*, his conviction was null. References to *Wood* and *Schenck*, and the legal arguments the cases raised, appeared again in Garrison's appeal to the U.S. Supreme Court.[7]

In a final attack on the defamation law's constitutionality, Organ examined the construction of the statute itself. The Louisiana Legislature had defined defamation too broadly, the attorney contended. Organ described the law as a "catch-all statute . . . which purports to restrain freedom of expression," and maintained it violated the U.S. Supreme Court decision in *Thornhill v. Alabama* (1940). In *Thornhill*, the court held such statutes "readily [lend themselves] to harsh and discriminatory enforcement by local prosecuting officials, against particular groups [that] merit their displeasure" and insisted that the laws resulted in "a continuous and pervasive restraint of all freedom of discussion." Therefore, Organ concluded, not only did the defamation law violate the First Amendment's free speech provisions, but its guarantees of freedom of expression as well. It was another way for Organ to raise the specter of sedition in his argument, and the U.S. Supreme Court addressed the statute's construction when it eventually overturned Garrison's conviction.[8]

The Louisiana Attorney General's Office filed a forty-five page brief in response to Garrison's appeal. In the document's opening pages, the state clearly intended to remind the justices of Garrison's culpability in the feud with the judges. The episode had resulted from the district attorney "falsely advising" Judge Shirley Wimberly that another judge had approved $900 from the fines and fees account for office furnishings when that was not the case. The state further contended that Garrison, angry over the limitations the judges had imposed on his office's funds, had waged a campaign of deception against the judges, which had reached its crescendo with his characterization of the judges as "sacred cows" and as sympathetic to vice operators. As it would throughout the appellate process, the state also noted that Garrison's attorneys had not called any of the twenty witnesses they had subpoenaed, nor had Garrison taken the stand to answer the charges against him. With these assertions, the Attorney General's Office suggested that Garrison had not mounted a defense to avoid answering questions that might embarrass him or expose him as dishonest.[9]

The remainder of the state's brief answered the bills of exception Garrison's attorneys had filed. Particularly noteworthy are the replies to the defense's assertions that Garrison's trial was unconstitutional and that the Louisiana defamation statutes violated the First Amendment's free speech guarantees. The state first attacked Garrison's complaint that trial Judge William Ponder had declined to recuse himself although statements by Attorney General Jack P.F. Gremillion had made the judge a plaintiff in the case. In response, the state insisted Ponder could not have recused himself, because to do so would have violated an order from the state Supreme Court, which had appointed him to hear the case because the case involved all the Orleans Parish Criminal Court judges. In answering Garrison's calls for a jury trial, the Attorney General's Office quoted a 1926 Louisiana Supreme Court ruling, *State v. Livaudais*, in which a defendant who faced a misdemeanor charge had questioned the lack of a jury trial. The court had upheld the provision in the state Constitution that allowed judges to hear misdemeanor cases. Based on that ruling, the state asserted, the defense's protest over a lack of a jury trial had no merit.[10]

The bulk of the brief was the state's response to Garrison's claim that the doctrine of qualified privilege, defined in Louisiana Revised Statute 14:49, protected his allegations against the judges. The statute specified that the privilege protects "statements regarding the conduct of persons in respect to public affairs . . . made in the reasonable belief of their truth." Garrison had claimed that his statements alleging the judges were sympathetic to racketeers had contained no malicious intent and had commented on their professional duties, not their personal lives. The state characterized this argument as "untenable," and further asserted that Garrison's statement "imputes moral turpitude to the eight judges, and accuses them of actions involving criminal conduct." Furthermore, Garrison had not provided any facts to prove the accuracy of his assertions, and, therefore, he could not claim qualified privilege as a defense, the state concluded.[11]

Nearly forty pages of Garrison's brief to the Louisiana Supreme Court attacked the state's defamation statute as a violation of the First Amendment's free speech protections, the appeal's major constitutional contention. Curiously, the attorney general's brief responded to this contention in less than three pages, and then only superficially. The state used a page and a half to dispute the defense's citation of *Wood v. Georgia* in its brief. The *Wood* case was a contempt charge, not a defamation case, and therefore its facts were irrelevant, the state alleged. The attorney general addressed the defamation statute's constitutionality indirectly but concisely, stating that the "Louisiana Constitution contains the safeguards of freedom of speech." The brief continued by citing Article 1, Section 3 of the Louisiana Constitution of 1921, which had defined protections for speech and for the press, and which, in the opinion of the attorney general, "is in no way inconsistent with Amendment One of the Constitution of the United States." Shortly after, the brief concluded much as it started— by reminding the justices that Garrison did not mount a defense or offer "one iota" of evidence to sustain his belief that his statements against the judges were true and not malicious.[12]

Attorney General Gremillion again used this assertion to cast doubt on Garrison's character when the Louisiana Supreme Court heard oral arguments in the case on May 3, 1963. All eight Orleans criminal court judges had testified at the lower court trial, Gremillion stated, but the district attorney had declined to take the stand and this had avoided questions regarding the accuracy of his statements. Donald Organ was not as fortunate—he could not dodge the justices' questions as he argued Garrison's appeal. The justices inquired if Organ believed Garrison's statements had demonstrated malice toward the judges. Predictably, Organ answered no. He believed the district attorney was commenting on public figures in their official capacity and therefore enjoyed qualified privilege. In a subsequent answer, Organ conceded that Garrison's comments might not have been in good taste, but insisted that impropriety alone did not demonstrate malice. From their remarks in open court, which indicated a belief that Garrison's statements indeed were malicious, the justices disagreed with Organ's assessment.[13]

As Garrison expected, the Louisiana Supreme Court upheld his conviction on June 4, 1963. Writing for the unanimous court, Associate Justice Walter B. Hamlin dismissed each of the twenty-six bills of exception Garrison's attorneys had filed. The bulk of the court's thirty-page opinion defended Louisiana's defamation statute, but Hamlin first rebutted Garrison's concerns that state law had denied him a jury trial, a violation of the Sixth Amendment to the U.S. Constitution. Previous Louisiana Supreme Court decisions decreed the Sixth Amendment applied only to violations of federal statutes, and ruled that the state government could prescribe the manner in which courts adjudicated trials, Hamlin wrote. Furthermore, in its opinion in *Betts v. Brady*, the U.S. Supreme Court had issued a similar statement supporting a state's right to decide the use of juries in misdemeanor cases. Garrison's attorneys had cited the March 1963 Supreme Court ruling decision in *Gideon v. Wainwright*, which overturned the earlier *Betts* decision, but Hamlin dismissed the defense's citation of the *Gideon* case because it dealt with the right to counsel, not a jury trial, and also involved a felony case, not a misdemeanor charge. Garrison "neither suffered prejudice nor deprivation of due process of law" because state law had denied him a jury trial, Hamlin concluded.[14]

In the opinion's remaining pages, Hamlin defended the constitutionality of Louisiana's defamation law and provided ample fodder for Garrison's later appeal to the U.S. Supreme Court. Hamlin relied extensively on the U.S. Supreme Court's decision in *Beauharnais v. Illinois* (1952), in which the court held that "libelous utterances are not within the area of constitutionally protected speech." In *Beauharnais*, the court had affirmed the "clear and present danger" precedent from the *Schenck* decision. Throughout the lower court trial and into the appeals process, Garrison's attorneys and the state prosecutors had argued over these two areas of the *Beauharnais* ruling. Trial Judge William Ponder had applied the first precedent, but had declined to utilize the "clear and present danger" standard. Now, the state Supreme Court agreed with Ponder and with Attorney General Gremillion's assessment that cases like *Schenck* that arose from contempt charges had no application in defamation proceedings. Hamlin wrote that the *Beauharnais* ruling, which eradicated First Amendment protection for libel and supported a state's right to punish libelous utterances, was appropriate to Garrison's appeal. Because he believed Garrison's statements against the judges were "defamatory" and were "made maliciously," Hamlin characterized them as libelous and therefore undeserving of First Amendment protection. The Louisiana Supreme Court's reliance on the *Beauharnais* ruling to affirm Garrison's conviction would later play a role in the U.S. Supreme Court's decision to review the district attorney's appeal.[15]

Reacting to the court's decision, an unsurprised and unapologetic Garrison said his defamation conviction "is not worth the paper on which it is written." The district attorney told reporters he was confident the U.S. Supreme Court would overturn his conviction "as an obvious violation of the United States Constitution." Before appealing the case to the nation's highest court, however, Garrison's attorneys sought a rehearing before the Louisiana Supreme Court. They contended Hamlin's ruling had dismissed several cases as inapplicable to their appeal, but had failed to give "serious consideration" to the arguments the precedents had posed. The attorneys also threatened to appeal to the U.S. Supreme Court if the state justices refused to rehear the case. They insisted the appeal would characterize the Louisiana defamation statute as analogous to a criminal sedition law. "The reason there is no United States Supreme Court decision—to date—involving the constitutionality of a state criminal libel statute . . . is that prosecutions for criminal libel are practically unheard of in this country," Organ wrote, adding that "prosecutions for seditious libel—or criminal libel of any kind" had disappeared nationwide. The modern use of criminal defamation laws would re-emerge when the U.S. Supreme Court considered Garrison's appeal.[16]

The state Supreme Court denied the application for a rehearing on June 28, 1963, and Garrison's attorneys immediately announced their intention to appeal to the U.S. Supreme Court. Although many of the defense's contentions would continue unchanged from those it made before the Louisiana Supreme Court, the district attorney remained certain that the outcome before the nation's highest court would be different.[17] To help ensure this, Garrison asked Eberhard P. Deutsch of New Orleans to act as his lead counsel. Although Organ had ably represented Garrison, Deutsch was an internationally renowned attorney who in the 1930s had formulated a First Amendment challenge to a newspaper advertising tax levied by the Louisiana Legislature at the behest of then-U.S. Senator Huey P. Long. The U.S. Supreme Court adopted many of Deutsch's arguments when it ruled in *Grosjean v. American Press Co.* (1936) that the tax violated press freedom. Deutsch's reputation as a legal scholar increased after the Second World War, when he helped establish a constitutional government in Austria. Garrison gave no public indication as to why he replaced Organ with Deutsch, but it is likely the district attorney believed Deutsch's reputation could only help his case.[18]

Deutsch's first task was to decide which path Garrison's case should take to the U.S. Supreme Court. Two options were available to him: certiorari or appeal. Under the court's rules, certain cases have a method of appeal assigned to them. For example, a case where a state invalidates a federal treaty or statute must arrive at the court by way of certiorari, a writ by which the Supreme Court orders an inferior court to produce the case's records. However, in cases where a state statute is questioned based on an issue of federal law, either certiorari or appeal is acceptable. Organ had laid ample groundwork—his arguments were replete with federal challenges to the state's defamation and jury trial statutes. Now, Deutsch simply had to choose the route.[19]

An attorney of Deutsch's experience knew that the court rejected far more certiorari requests than appeals. In an appeal, an attorney provided the pertinent facts of the case through a jurisdictional statement, a booklet that outlined the case's history and the legal reasons the court should grant a review. In certiorari, the court had the option to review the entire record, but routinely dismissed certiorari requests because it did not believe the attorneys raised substantive questions that would merit initiating the lengthy process. A respected guidebook for court practitioners offered an answer to the question

Deutsch now faced: "In situations where either appeal or certiorari is clearly proper, it is advisable to take the appeal." Deutsch did so and began to craft a jurisdictional statement that would demonstrate that Garrison's case involved a federal question that the court had yet to consider. Deutsch also would have to show that the Louisiana Supreme Court's ruling conflicted with previous decisions by the U.S. Supreme Court.[20]

Deutsch completed a one hundred and forty-page jurisdictional statement by mid-July 1963. In it, he amplified many of Organ's previous contentions. If the court granted the appeal, he would have more time to formulate his own arguments. He began the appeal by recounting that Garrison's November 2, 1962, statements criticizing the criminal court judges were in response to Judge William O'Hara's comments the previous day. Unlike Organ, who had mentioned it only in passing, Deutsch stressed the idea that O'Hara had provoked Garrison. Furthermore, the attorney asserted that Garrison's comments "related solely to the Judge's [sic] official conduct. At no point did it refer to the private conduct of any of them." Obviously, Deutsch was again asserting the doctrine of qualified privilege into the argument, something Organ had done as well. The bulk of the appeal repeated Organ's contention that the Louisiana defamation statute allowed sedition prosecutions. The Supreme Court had yet to consider such a case, Deutsch claimed, "despite its obvious and elemental importance." The Louisiana law that defined defamation as a misdemeanor, and therefore as ineligible for a jury trial, only made the situation more egregious and deserving of the court's consideration, Deutsch contended. He further insisted that the Louisiana Supreme Court misinterpreted the U.S. Supreme Court's *Schenck* and *Beauharnais* decisions when it upheld trial Judge William Ponder's refusal to apply the "clear and present danger" test to Garrison's statements. Deutsch would continue to assert similar arguments as the appeal continued.[21]

In its thirty-two page response, the Louisiana Attorney General's Office attempted to convince the justices that neither the state's defamation law nor its jury trial statute violated federal law; therefore, Garrison's case did not merit review. In its jurisdictional statement, Garrison's defense had insisted that the trial judge had erred by not applying the *Schenck* "clear and present danger" test to the district attorney's statements. As it had before the state Supreme Court, the Attorney General's Office again contended that the *Schenck* standard applied only to contempt cases and not defamation charges. "In our opinion, [Garrison] has made a deliberate effort to confuse this court by implying there is no distinction," the brief stated, continuing, "Contempt is essentially an offense against the orderly administration of justice, while defamation is essentially a crime against society involving injury to individual human beings." Furthermore, the attorney general's brief argued that the state court was correct in its assertion that Garrison's statements, as libel, deserved no constitutional protection citing the U.S. Supreme Court's *Beauharnais* decision and its ruling in *Chaplinsky v. New Hampshire* (1942). In *Chaplinsky*, the court ruled that defamatory statements could incite the public and that states had the right to curtail such utterances without threatening freedom of speech. Among the terms that the court characterized as "fighting words" in its *Chaplinsky* ruling was "racketeer," the brief argued. The state concluded its argument by again mentioning that Garrison had not taken the stand in his own defense and reiterated its argument that the district attorney's statements were not a fair comment on the judges' official conduct but rather a "purely personal abuse."[22]

The state's arguments failed to convince a majority of the justices, who granted Garrison's appeal on November 12, 1963. Associate justices Arthur J. Goldberg Jr., Byron R. White, William J. Brennan Jr., William O. Douglas, Hugo L. Black, and Chief Justice Earl Warren voted to add the case to the court's calendar for the October 1963 term, then underway. Justices Potter Stewart, John Marshall Harlan II, and Tom C. Clark voted to deny the appeal. News that the high court would consider his case perhaps provided a sense of vindication for Garrison, who that very week was locked in yet another verbal tussle, this time with the New Orleans Bar Association. Four days before the Supreme Court granted the appeal, the association released the findings of its inquiry into the parish prison overcrowding, the situation that had inspired Garrison's description of the judges as "sacred cows." The report urged the District Attorney's Office to set trial dates more quickly and also recommended that the judges take one month of vacation annually, rather than two and half months. The association concluded that a harmonious relationship between the judges and the prosecutor could reduce the prison population. "If the interested parties responsible for the administration of justice were to put aside personal differences and avoid public incriminating or derogatory statements, they would have more time to give to the discharge of duties required by their oaths of office," the report insisted.[23]

Garrison called the bar association's report "useless and misleading" and mocked its admonitions as "sanctimonious," claiming: "The disagreement between the district attorney's office and the judges, as a group, has long since been replaced by a good working relationship." Garrison's statements dripped with disgust for the New Orleans legal community, which he characterized as having "its head buried in the sand," reflecting his own belief that he could not expect impartiality and fairness from the Louisiana judicial system. The criminal court judges charged him with defamation. A jurist from another parish found him guilty. The justices of the state's highest court affirmed that decision. Now, the city's largest group of lawyers was calling him ineffective, when he believed he orchestrated "the historic increase of productive time in the last year both on the part of the courts and the district attorney's office." Nevertheless, as his case moved into its final stage before the nation's highest judicial body, Garrison remained certain that the U.S. Supreme Court would overturn his conviction and finally silence his critics.[24]

While Garrison continued to fight battles locally, his lawyers had elevated his case beyond its genesis as a conflict over money and political power. Garrison's defamation conviction had come at the end of a four-day trial bent on embarrassing the criminal court judges, his accusers. His attorneys had abandoned that strategy in favor of an appeal that asked serious constitutional questions about the right of defendants to a jury trial and, more important, the place of criticism in a democracy. These far-reaching arguments carried the case through the appeals process and removed the taint of local partisan politics that had characterized its origins.

CHAPTER IV

Supreme Struggle:
The Justices Confront *Garrison*

Law clerk Francis X. Beytagh pulled another appeal from the stack on his desk. The Supreme Court had received nearly 2,300 petitions for the October 1963 term, and Beytagh and his fellow clerks were responsible for sifting through them all and preparing memoranda for their boss, Earl Warren, the chief justice of the United States. Warren had one rule for his clerks: Keep the memoranda they prepared for his review as brief as possible. Beytagh undoubtedly recalled the maxim as he scanned Jim Garrison's one hundred forty-page jurisdictional statement, a booklet outlining his appeal's pertinent constitutional questions. After reading the document and the Louisiana Attorney General's response, Beytagh placed a six-by-four inch piece of paper in his typewriter and commenced writing a ten-page summary for the chief. It began: "This case presents the question whether a state can convict an individual of criminal libel for allegedly derogatory remarks made and published about official conduct of certain state (court) judges, without jury trial, without violating his constitutionally protected right of free speech." This was the first time the Supreme Court had confronted such a question.[1]

Clerks for the court's other eight members performed similar tasks as well, and the memos served as the justices' introduction to Garrison's case. These modest beginnings—a collection of law clerks and their typewriters—soon gave way to the intricate operations of the nation's highest judicial body. Over the next year, the court wrestled with the central question Garrison's appeal raised—if state defamation laws served any modern utility other than to suppress criticism and unpopular speech. This question elevated the case beyond its origins as a local dispute over money and political influence; the appeal now had the potential to expand free speech nationwide. Yet because of the malevolent foundations of Garrison's appeal, the justices struggled to determine the degree to which the First Amendment protected a citizen's right to criticize the job performances of elected officials. The court twice considered the case, and the jus-

tices produced nearly thirty draft opinions, hundreds of pages that
exemplified the difficulty in deciding what merit, if any, the appeal
had. Garrison's defamation conviction had resulted from a fight with
a group of judges, now his fate ironically rested with another group
of jurists—and the outcome was far from certain. Nevertheless, by
November 1964, with its long deliberative process completed, the
court used Garrison's appeal to cement its two-phased alteration of
the nation's libel laws and, in the process, to expand public discourse
in the United States. The first step was *New York Times v. Sullivan*; the
second was *Garrison v. Louisiana*.[2]

The court's study of Garrison's appeal began with the clerks. Like
Warren's aide Beytagh, most were recent law school graduates. The
chief justice and many of the court's other members delegated immense responsibilities to their clerks, including sorting the appeals
and making recommendations on how the court should proceed. In
the simple, jargon-free style Warren favored, Beytagh began his summary of Garrison's appeal and guided the chief justice through the
case's background—the crusade against vice on New Orleans' Bourbon Street, the dispute with the parish's criminal court judges over
funding, the district attorney's statements calling the jurists ineffi-
cient, and his allegations that the judges were beholden to racketeers.
The clerk noted that the Louisiana Supreme Court had upheld Garrison's conviction based on *Beauharnais v. Illinois* (1952), in which the
U.S. Supreme Court had ruled that libelous statements did not fall
under the protection of the First Amendment's free speech clause.
In *Beauharnais*, the court had affirmed its 1919 ruling in *Schenck v.
U.S.*, which had established the "clear and present danger" standard
to judge the criminality of words. However, *Schenck* was the result
of a contempt charge, and the Louisiana courts had claimed the distinction between contempt and defamation removed the necessity of
applying the "clear and present danger" test to Garrison's conviction.
Beytagh characterized the failure to do so as central to Garrison's appeal.[3]

It was Warren's practice to examine his clerks' memoranda in the
quiet of his home. He would go over them and underline in pencil
details he thought especially compelling. On Beytagh's memo, Warren marked several passages that indicated the chief justice's inclina-

tion to re-examine the *Beauharnais* precedent and the *Schenck* "clear and present danger" standard. "[Garrison] contends that [Louisiana] cannot constitutionally convict him of criminal libel," the chief underscored, "when his statement plainly involved no clear and present danger, either to the preservation of the peace or to the proper administration of justice." Beytagh conceded that if the court considered the appeal based on the *Beauharnais* precedent denying libel the protection of the First Amendment, it likely would uphold Garrison's conviction. However, the clerk could not understand how the lower court had applied this part of the *Beauharnais* precedent, but refused to utilize the "clear and present danger" stipulation. "This seems rather cockeyed to me," Beytagh insisted. "I realize that criminal libel laws are of ancient vintage, but I doubt their modern utility and feel rather strongly that they are presently little more than an anachronistic survival of days far antedating of our bill of rights [*sic*]." He recommended the chief justice vote to grant Garrison's appeal. When the justices met on November 12, 1963, Warren joined justices William J. Brennan Jr., Hugo L. Black, William O. Douglas, Byron R. White, and Arthur J. Goldberg Jr. in voting to place Garrison's case on the court's calendar. Justices Tom C. Clark, John Marshall Harlan II, and Potter Stewart opposed the appeal.[4]

After it agreed to review the case, the court required Garrison's lawyers and the Louisiana Attorney General's Office to file briefs restating their positions. Both litigants largely reaffirmed statements made in previous court filings. As he had in the previous year's jurisdictional statement, Garrison's attorney Eberhard P. Deutsch again characterized the Louisiana defamation statute as a disguised sedition law. In the brief he filed with the court on February 14, 1964, Deutsch insisted that the *Schenck* "clear and present danger" rule was a meager safeguard against libel prosecutions, especially if a court refused to apply the provision, as the trial court had in Garrison's case. The Louisiana Supreme Court had held that the "clear and present danger" test applied only to contempt cases and not to defamation prosecutions. Deutsch insisted the Louisiana court had believed illogically "that the constitutional protection established by [the U.S. Supreme Court] can be circumvented merely by denominating a prosecution 'criminal libel' rather than 'contempt of court.'" A lower court's refusal to apply the standard should compel the justices to re-examine both *Schenck* and *Beauharnais*, Deutsch argued, particularly the condition in the latter case that eradicated First Amendment protection for libelous speech. Garrison's attorney characterized the *Beauharnais* decision as "erroneous" and urged the court to use his client's case either to overturn the precedent or to clarify that the First Amendment protected an individual's right to criticize government. "Any interest of the State in protecting the reputations of its officers must yield to the higher First Amendment interest in unfettered discussion of their official conduct," Deutsch asserted. To supplement his argument, Deutsch mingled passages from preeminent First Amendment scholars Thomas I. Emerson and Zechariah Chafee with quotations from Thomas Jefferson and James Madison, all of whom believed that criminal libel prosecutions were analogous to trials for sedition. Criminal defamation statutes like Louisiana's allowed for sedition trials and deserved evaluation by the court, Deutsch concluded. "The only way in which speech can be protected adequately against governmental restriction is by striking down all statutes whose aim is punishment of speech as defamation," he insisted.[5]

After establishing his belief that Garrison's trial was an unconstitutional prosecution for sedition, Deutsch again argued—as he had in previous court documents—that the Louisiana law denying his client a jury trial exacerbated the situation. Louisiana law did not require jury trials for misdemeanor offenses such as defamation, but Deutsch characterized a jury as a safeguard against seditious libel prosecutions, especially if the courts refused to apply the "clear and present danger" rule. Deutsch was not only attacking the Louisiana law that denied Garrison a jury trial, as previous filings had. He now attempted to convince the justices that the Louisiana courts had infringed twice on his client's rights, first by ignoring the U.S. Supreme Court's "clear and present danger" test and second by denying him a jury trial. Deutsch concluded that the lack of a jury as a safety net all but assured a guilty verdict.[6]

The jury safeguard served not only as a check on the government's power to prosecute its critics but also to encourage an open discourse that might include unpopular ideas, Deutsch continued. Throughout his brief, Deutsch argued positions he knew would find favor with certain justices. For example, the attorney's arguments against seditious libel appealed to justices Hugo L. Black and William O. Douglas, both of whom consistently espoused an absolutist view of the First Amendment. Once during an interview, Black famously said that when the First Amendment mandated that Congress "make no law" infringing on free speech, it meant *no* law. Similarly, as he argued that unpopular speech demanded a higher degree of First Amendment protection, Deutsch may have had in mind a view Justice William J. Brennan Jr. once expressed. In his opinion in *Roth v. U.S.* (1957), Brennan wrote: "All ideas having even the slightest redeeming social importance—unorthodox ideas, controversial ideas, even ideas hateful to the prevailing climate of opinion—have the full protection" of the First Amendment. In a passage that echoed Brennan's *Roth* opinion, Deutsch suggested that no constitutional protection for popular speech was necessary, while controversial ideas needed the First Amendment's full embrace. "To limit the free-speech guarantees to what the majority considers right, would be to hobble, not to aid, the search for the truth, and thereby to defeat the whole beneficent purpose" of the First Amendment, he concluded. In his attempt to appeal to the different justices' established positions, Deutsch demonstrated a detailed knowledge of the court's history. He also hoped to provide some ease to the justices' deliberations of Garrison's case, but those negotiations would be far from easy.[7]

The Louisiana Attorney General's response differed sharply in both style and substance from Deutsch's brief. The state's brief, written primarily by Assistant Attorney General Michael E. Culligan, set out to convince the justices that they had granted Garrison's appeal erroneously. Furthermore, Culligan intended to cast aspersions on the district attorney's integrity. To achieve the latter goal, the assistant attorney general used homey language and peculiar aphorisms that contrasted sharply from the scholarly tenor of Deutsch's brief. Culligan opened with several colorful passages that were clearly aimed at calling Garrison's motives and character into question. While Deutsch's brief attempted to portray his client in the light of a heroic, crusading prosecutor, Culligan alleged that Garrison "embarked upon a career of public speaking and the spending of public funds" after he became Orleans Parish district attorney in May 1962. He further characterized Garrison's expenditures on office furnishings from the fines and fees account as excessive and lauded the judges' decision to halt his spending. "Their apprehension was well founded, for it was [Garrison's] attitude that the fund was his to spend in any way he saw fit and that it was his duty to spend it as fast as possible," Culligan wrote. He described Garrison's response to the judicial funding roadblock as "filled with venom" and as "spewing hatred like an avenging Fury." Garrison clearly intended to strike at the judges' personal reputations when he had linked them publicly with criminals, and Culligan concluded that such malicious and uncivil behavior did not deserve First Amendment protection.[8]

The remainder of Culligan's brief attempted to convince the Supreme Court justices that Deutsch had misled them into erroneously granting Garrison's appeal. Culligan focused on four arguments to dissect Garrison's case. The first hammered at the contention that the Louisiana defamation statute was a camouflaged sedition law. The Louisiana Legislature had defined defamation, contempt of court, and sedition as three separate and distinct offenses, Culligan argued. Under Louisiana law, sedition involved disruption of government, but Garrison's comments had only impugned the judges' personal reputations, he explained. The state did not enforce its defamation law to punish criticism, but rather to deter crime, Culligan maintained. Again employing homespun aphorisms, the assistant attorney general suggested the defamation statute merely reflected civilized society's intolerance for primitive acts of retributive violence. "In early times, if someone put out your eye, you waylaid him and knocked his brains out," Culligan stated, continuing, "if someone destroyed your reputation, you waylaid him and committed mayhem." The Louisiana law dissuaded such acts, and Culligan rebuffed the assertions of those who claimed civilized society did not need such laws. "Perhaps a member of that infinitesimally small segment of our society known as the intellectual elite would not resort to violence for vengeance if he were called a racketeer," he insisted, continuing, "A state cannot create classifications within its criminal libel statute by providing that intellectuals and judges are not pugnacious, whereas truckdrivers and prizefighters are." Considering Culligan was making an argument to the justices of the U.S. Supreme Court, several of whom considered themselves intellectuals, these were odd assertions for the brief to make. Furthermore, Culligan's brief seemed to disregard the court's own rules for filings, which mandated lawyers remove "burdensome, irrelevant, immaterial, and scandalous manner," and restrict arguments to clear points of law.[9] The remainder of the state's brief fortunately contained few similarly strange inferences. In the second of four points of contention aimed at refuting Garrison's argument, Culligan again repeated the state's belief that the lower court's refusal to apply the "clear and present" danger standard to Garrison's defamatory statements was correct. The "clear and present danger" test applied only to contempt proceedings, the state insisted, and therefore was not applicable to Garrison's defamation charge because Louisiana law treated contempt and defamation as distinct charges. The defamation statute furthermore allowed punishment for libelous utterances. Therefore, it stood to reason that the Louisiana Legislature, in drafting the law, took into account the danger associated with defamatory statements, Culligan reasoned. "Clear and present danger therefore has no application," in Garrison's appeal because, "the legislative body itself has previously determined the danger," he concluded. Finally, Culligan argued the Legislature had written the statute in such a way to allow for an uninhibited discussion of public issues, but had agreed that the First Amendment did not shield defamatory statements or block a state from punishing offenders.[10]

The third and fourth sections of the state's brief attempted to convince the court that the case involved no federal questions and therefore fell outside of the Supreme Court's jurisdiction. Garrison's attorneys had contended the state had infringed on his right to a jury trial guaranteed in the Sixth Amendment to the U.S. Constitution. Not so, Culligan responded. The Sixth Amendment applied only to federal prosecutions and did not mandate that a state try every offense in front of a jury. In its final section, the brief repeated its contention that both the Louisiana defamation statute and the Louisiana Constitution protected a person's right to criticize public officials and were, therefore, harmonious with the First Amendment's free speech guarantees. Culligan pointed out that in several decisions—notably *Beauharnais* and *Chaplinsky v. New Hampshire* (1942)—the U.S. Supreme Court had held that a state could prosecute defamation cases without infringing on the First Amendment, which the court had further asserted did not protect libel in the first place. In these rulings, Culligan concluded, the court had upheld a state's right to protect its citizens "from the evils of malicious, libelous utterances," like those for which the state had prosecuted Garrison.[11]

The Louisiana Attorney General's Office filed its brief with the Supreme Court's clerk on March 9, 1964, the same day the justices ruled in *New York Times v. Sullivan*, an opinion seminal to the court's *Garrison* decision eight months later. The *Times* case stemmed from a lawsuit filed by L.B. Sullivan, the former Montgomery, Alabama, commissioner of public affairs, against the *New York Times*, which had published a pro-civil rights advertisement in March 1960. Although his name had not appeared in the advertisement, Sullivan alleged the ad contained several incorrect statements that defamed him in his official capacity as the head of the Montgomery Police Department. A jury awarded Sullivan $500,000 in damages, and the Alabama Supreme Court affirmed the ruling. The U.S. Supreme Court agreed to hear the case.[12]

The decision the Supreme Court announced in March 1964 established for the first time that the First Amendment protected statements critical of public officials. The *Times* ruling overturned previous court precedents in *Beauharnais v. Illinois* and other cases that had placed libel outside of the First Amendment's protection. With the *Times* ruling, the court redefined the nation's libel laws, and for Garrison and his attorneys, the landmark decision provided a solid foundation under which they could characterize the Louisiana defamation statute as a violation of the First Amendment.[13]

The *Times* ruling did not allow libelous statements to be made with impunity, however. Writing for the court, Associate Justice William J. Brennan Jr. suggested that earlier court decisions on libel had not satisfied the First Amendment's free speech guarantees. Libel, Brennan wrote, was not immune from constitutional limitations, but the court should establish a standard to ensure, in one of the ruling's most famous phrases, "that debate on public issues should be uninhibited, robust, and wide-open." Then Brennan repeated a sentiment that he had set forth in the court's *Roth* ruling and to which Deutsch alluded in his brief in the *Garrison* case. An "uninhibited" public discourse "may well include vehement, caustic, and sometimes unpleasantly sharp attacks on government and public officials," the justice insisted in his *Times* opinion. The First Amendment protected the right to criticize the Montgomery Police Department's official actions, although the ad had contained several misstatements of fact, Brennan wrote. To add historical relevance to the decision, the justice then quoted James Madison's sentiments regarding the Sedition Act of 1798 that the father of the Bill of Rights had included in his *Virginia Resolutions*. In a statement that Deutsch also cited in his brief to the court, Madison wrote: "Some degree of abuse is inseparable from the proper use of every thing; and in no instance is this more true than in that of the press." In short, Brennan insisted neither error in fact nor injury to reputation overwhelmed the constitutional right to free speech. Furthermore, the justice concluded that to limit speech on those grounds would effectively re-establish sedition laws and would result in self-censorship that "dampens the vigor and limits the variety of public debate."[14]

Up to this point, Brennan's *Times* ruling mirrored several of the sentiments Deutsch had suggested in his *Garrison* brief, but the associate justice went further. The Supreme Court had for too long dodged an acceptable measure of libel, Brennan asserted. Previous rulings had merely dismissed libel as injurious to the First Amendment, but with such statements, the court had unwittingly limited free speech. The *Times* decision afforded the court a vehicle to remove the ambiguity that had governed libel law since the early days of the republic, Brennan insisted, and in a single paragraph, he provided a clear test to determine whether statements critical of public officials were constitutionally sound.

> The constitutional guarantees require, we think, a federal rule that prohibits a public official from recovering damages for a defamatory falsehood relating to his official conduct unless he proves that the statement was made with "actual malice"—that is, with knowledge that it was false or with reckless disregard of whether it was false or not.[15]

The actual malice rule eradicated the ambiguous "clear and present danger" doctrine that served as the standard to evaluate libelous statements since the *Schenck* decision in 1919. Previous court decisions placed an extreme burden of proof on defendants charged with libel. Now, the court transferred the load to the plaintiffs. More important, the *Times* decision severely limited a state's ability to grant civil damages to public officials who characterized criticism of their job performance as libelous. This element of the *Times* ruling would be decisive as the sides in the *Garrison* case reworked their arguments to conform to the court's ruling.[16]

After the *Times* decision, Deutsch believed he needed more time to reformulate his arguments given the developments in libel law, and he asked the court to postpone hearing Garrison's appeal. The court denied the request, and Deutsch, despite his desire for additional time, filed a supplemental brief with the court less than a month after the *Times* ruling. The document differed greatly from his previous court filings. Neither in the jurisdictional statement nor in his initial brief had Deutsch allowed for the possibility that Garrison's statements against the judges had been false. Although he used arguments from James Madison, among others, that some misstatement of fact was inevitable in public discourse, Deutsch had not relied on that contention to the extent he did in the supplemental brief. Under the new doctrine established in the *Times* decision, Deutsch could attack Garrison's conviction using the parameters of the court's ruling that granted false statements made without malice the protection of the First Amendment. Deutsch no longer had to rely on the ambiguous nature of the "clear and present danger" precedent. Using Brennan's opinion, he now had a clear definition under which to exonerate his client. He simply had to demonstrate that Garrison's statements were not malicious—whether they were untrue or not became secondary. During Garrison's trial, the state used public comments the district attorney made throughout his row with the judges to prove malice. Deutsch now insisted the statements had not reflected personal malice, but rather animosity toward the judges' official conduct. When considered as a whole, Garrison's statements regarding the judges' excessive vacations, the backlog of untried cases, and the halting of funds for his vice campaign demonstrated "an absence of personal animosity on his part toward the judges," Deutsch wrote. He further suggested that the district attorney's desire to make the public aware of problems within the judicial system had inspired his comments. Whether they were true or false now became incidental under the new guidelines the court had established in *Times*, Deutsch concluded.[17]

Deutsch began and concluded the supplemental brief by suggesting that the *Times* ruling had addressed many of the issues in his client's appeal. In its responding brief, the Louisiana Attorney General's Office discounted the comparison between the two cases. Again writing for the state, Assistant Attorney General Culligan established two significant differences between the cases. The first noted that the newspaper advertisement at the center of the *Times* case had mentioned no one by name. Garrison left little doubt about whom he was speaking when he alleged racketeer influences on "our eight vacation-minded judges," Culligan explained. He conceded that some of Garrison's comments regarding the judges had been in reference to their official conduct, but insisted that the "accusation of racketeer influence went beyond criticism of official conduct and attacked the worth of the persons who were judges as individuals and attacked their personal reputations." Culligan also refuted Deutsch's claim that Garrison's comments contained no malice toward the judges and only demonstrated his desire to make the public aware of faults in the parish judicial system. He referred to this defense as a "subterfuge for a vengeful attack" on the personal reputations of the eight criminal court judges.[18]

Culligan then described the second difference; the record in *Times* indicated no actual malice on the part of the defendants. Garrison, however, "knew what he said was a falsehood when he deliberately set out to injure the reputations of every one of the eight individuals who were Criminal Court judges," Culligan insisted. The Supreme Court had found no malice in the *Times* case. If the court considered the record of Garrison's lower court trial, however, it would find evidence that Garrison "made the accusation of 'racketeer influence' knowing that it was false or with a reckless disregard to whether it was false or not," Culligan wrote, using the court's definition of actual malice to punctuate his point. He concluded his brief with a fact the state had repeated throughout the appeals process—that Garrison's attorneys had rested their case without mounting a defense. The state's final swat at Garrison's credibility would emerge again as the appeal moved into the oral arguments phase.[19]

The court scheduled oral arguments for April 22, 1964, and allotted one half hour for each side to present its case. The abbreviated period forced attorneys to summarize their cases' most important merits while leaving time for questions from the justices. Although the Supreme Court's rules limited the time lawyers had to make their presentations, it dictated no such restrictions on the justices' ability to ask questions. There was no pattern for questioning; justices simply interrupted a lawyer with an inquiry or comment at any time. As Deutsch approached the court's rostrum to begin his argument, he faced nine justices known for their vigorous examination of lawyers appearing before them. At the center of the long bench was Chief Justice Warren. Seating for the remaining associate justices alternated from right to left based on seniority. Black, the most senior justice, sat at Warren's right hand. Douglas, who like Black was appointed to the court by President Franklin D. Roosevelt, sat to Warren's left. Black and Douglas represented the court's most ardent supporters of unencumbered free speech, a fact Deutsch knew well. At the bench's far left was White, appointed by President John F. Kennedy and in his second year on court. Next to him sat Brennan, the author of the *Times* decision and one of four remaining appointees selected by President Dwight D. Eisenhower. Clark, with whom Deutsch had corresponded since 1947 when the justice was President Harry Truman's attorney general, sat between Brennan and Black. To Warren's left was Douglas, then John Marshall Harlan II, grandson of an associate justice of the same name and another Eisenhower appointee. Stewart, a fourth Eisenhower selection, and Goldberg, Kennedy's final appointee, occupied the remaining two seats. With these nine men rested the outcome of Garrison's appeal, and Deutsch would have to convince at least five of them that his client's conviction deserved a reversal.[20]

Warren announced the case, number four hundred on the court's docket, and then signaled to Deutsch to begin his argument. The attorney focused immediately on his belief that the Supreme Court should reverse Garrison's conviction based on the actual malice doctrine the court had established in the *Times* decision. Deutsch's contentions were semantic. Trial Judge William Ponder had suggested in his opinion that the state had proved actual malice, but, Deutsch argued, Louisiana's definition of malice and the court's characterization of malice differed. Furthermore, the Louisiana defamation statutes allowed the state to punish libelous statements not based on their falsity, but rather if they had been made with malice. The state merely needed to demonstrate malice to convict; whether the statements were true was no defense. "In other words, even if Garrison had a reasonable belief in the truth of what he was saying, [Ponder] still [found] he was actuated by malice," Deutsch explained to the justices, insisting, "He's not talking about your kind of malice." Garrison's attorney then attempted to move on, but Justice Brennan questioned Deutsch's contention that his client's case was similar in scope to the court's *Times* ruling. Brennan asked if Louisiana's definition of malice differed significantly enough from the *Times* classification to warrant a reversal. Yes, Deutsch answered. The justice pressed the lawyer again—were the two standards incongruent enough to compel the court to reverse Garrison's conviction? Deutsch then provided the answer Brennan seemed to want:

> Deutsch: You see, in the *Times* case, *you didn't make a finding in regard to a criminal case at all.* You were talking about the right of a public official to recover civil damages.[21]
>
> Brennan: I am only assuming, from what you have suggested, that we should agree with you . . . what I am trying to get to, is whether you think there is a sufficient departure from the *Times* test of malice that you would be entitled on that ground alone, assuming that the *Times* test applied, to a reversal.
>
> Deutsch: I stand on that.
> Brennan: You do?
> Deutsch: Yes.[22]

No one in the marbled courtroom could know it, but Brennan's line of questioning foretold the very element that would elevate the *Garrison* case to landmark status. In its eventual ruling, the Supreme Court would restrict a state's ability to use libel laws as a means to suppress criticism by extending the *Times* actual malice standard to include criminal as well as civil cases.[23]

Deutsch used the remainder of his half-hour allotment to attack the constitutionality of sedition statutes. State libel laws, especially when used to punish criticism of official conduct, "simply cannot be reconciled" with the First Amendment's free speech guarantees, he told the justices. Garrison's criticism of the overcrowded jail situation and the judges' vacation schedule were not actuated by malice, but rather by civic duty, Deutsch contended. The statements targeted professional, not personal, behavior, and for the state to punish him for such criticism amounted to a sedition charge. One of the justices then questioned Deutsch as to his client's belief that all eight judges were under the sway of racketeers—did not that comment alone prove malice?[24] Deutsch avoided a direct answer and instead argued that Garrison simply had raised the question of racketeer influence, but never said definitively that the judges were sympathetic to criminal elements.[25]

This response drew a comment of support from Justice Black, who had expressed his discomfort with the actual malice rule since the court's *Times* decision. How, the justice asked Deutsch, were the courts to determine malice? "It is a common, ordinary thing for a man to think that someone else who violently disagrees with a view that he violently holds either has to be dishonest or a fool," Black explained, asking, "How are you going to get down into the knowledge [of] what a man absolutely knew? What are the facts on which he based that statement?" Black did not intend for Deutsch to answer the question, but he posed it to assert again his belief that the actual malice test fell short of his absolutist view of the First Amendment—that free speech could be considered truly free only when the court protected public discourse from libel prosecutions, seditious and otherwise. For the purposes of his client's case, Deutsch could not agree more.[26]

After answering a few additional questions, Deutsch ceded the rostrum to Louisiana Attorney General Jack P.F. Gremillion. Gremillion's approach to oral arguments diverged sharply from Deutsch's. Deutsch appeared affable, prepared, and conciliatory. Gremillion was confrontational and spoke in a manner that befitted a stump speech, but that seemed out of place in the nation's highest court. The attorney general attempted early in his presentation to recount the case's origins in a manner that again questioned Garrison's character. He recalled how Garrison went from one judge to the next to receive approval for his expenditures. He also mentioned at least three times in his half-hour argument that Garrison had not mounted a defense at his lower court trial. The justices seemed disinclined to discuss Gremillion's *ad hominem* attack, all of which the state had included in its filings with the court in the hopes of darkening Garrison's personal integrity. Instead, the jurists asked Gremillion if Louisiana's defamation statute allowed sedition prosecutions. Furthermore, the justices inquired, had not Garrison merely criticized the judges' official conduct? They also wanted to know why the state had declined to apply the "clear and present danger" test to measure Garrison's statements. "We have no clear and present danger involved in this matter because there was no . . . obstruction of justice" or breakdown in the Orleans Parish judicial system resulting from Garrison's statements, Gremillion answered. Nevertheless, he contended the state had a duty to punish the district attorney's statements ridiculing "the personal reputation of these judges. These men happened to be judges and he defamed them in their personal category." Justice Brennan then interrupted the attorney general. "Now, Mr. Attorney General, would it be conceivable that [Garrison] would have said these things if [the judges] were not in office?" Brennan asked. Gremillion conceded: "Oh, absolutely not, he would have had no occasion to." Chief Justice Warren then asked Gremillion to pinpoint what in Garrison's statements referred only to the judges' personal reputations and not to their official conduct. Gremillion answered that Garrison's criticisms related to jail overcrowding and to a mounting docket; because the judges had nothing to do with either of these things, the district attorney's statements against them were personal, not professional. He continued:

> [In his statement on November 2, 1962, Garrison] said that all of these things, about the backlog of these cases . . . about the crowded conditions of the jail. These judges have nothing to do with that—the criminal sheriff is in charge of the jail, the district attorney in Louisiana has complete charge of the docket. He determines who comes to trial, when he comes to trial, and how he will

prosecute it. All of those statements in here are absolutely
false and we proved them as false. . . . The statements of
official conduct was conduct that these judges had nothing to do with.[27]

Gremillion's answer seemed insufficient to Warren, providing a hint
that the chief justice was likely to favor a reversal, as he eventually did.
The attorney general's statement also indicated that Gremillion was
uncertain of a key tenet of the *Times* malice standard—that whether
Garrison made his allegations with malice was now more important
than whether the statements were true. This ignorance later returned
to haunt Gremillion.[28]

Gremillion's presentation injected levity into the usually stoic
court. In his attempt to prove that Garrison's statements had subjected the judges to public ridicule, the attorney general recounted
the testimony of Criminal District Judge Edward A. Haggerty Jr., who
claimed that after Garrison's "sacred cow" comments, cries of "Moo!
Moo! Moo!" had greeted him when he had entered the New Orleans
Athletic Club. Gremillion shouted each "Moo!" into the rostrum mi-
crophone, drawing laughter from the gallery and the justices. Another
Orleans Parish judge had testified that his son's classmate had told the
boy his father was a "crook." Justice Stewart asked Gremillion: "Was
that boy tried for defamation?" When Gremillion told the justices
that Garrison had predicted that the Supreme Court would overturn
his conviction, Justice Douglas, who had remained silent throughout
the oral arguments, looked up from the bench and asked him, "Did he
say if it would be a unanimous vote?"[29]

Lightheartedness soon gave way to discomfort. Near the end of
his presentation, the justices barraged Gremillion with questions that
resulted in the attorney general defending himself rather than prosecuting Garrison. When the attorney general announced that "there
is a lot of vice" on New Orleans' Bourbon Street, Chief Justice Warren, a former prosecutor and attorney general himself, asked Gremillion if he, as Louisiana's top law enforcement officer, could not step in
to quell illegal activity there. Gremillion hedged and said he did not
make it a practice to supersede district attorneys and police chiefs.
Why then, another justice asked, had he stepped in to prosecute
Garrison? "I think the interest of the state is . . . the honesty of these

men was at stake and if they had been guilty of racketeer influences, they had no business serving on that bench," the attorney general answered. The justices then questioned Gremillion as to the number of defamation prosecutions in Louisiana. He replied he knew of twenty-five or thirty, but not all of them related to the conduct of judges. "I take it there are statements made in Louisiana about judges, state and federal," Justice White inquired. Gremillion answered:

> Oh, there are plenty of statements . . . I have heard [the U.S. Supreme Court] criticized quite precipitously in Louisiana, but no one has said you are influenced by racketeers, and nobody has called you sacred cows, or said you belonged to an association of armed robbers.[30]

The final exchange, while nebulous enough in content, had definite controversial undertones. The justices were well aware, as was at least one newspaper reporter in the press gallery, of Gremillion's past criticisms of the federal court system. During the New Orleans integration crisis in 1960, a federal district court had filed contempt charges against the attorney general for storming out of a hearing. "I'm not going to stay in this den of iniquity," Gremillion had shouted as he headed for the door, pausing his retreat long enough to spit on a group of black parents seated in the rear of the courtroom. Gremillion continued his protest in the corridor, pacing the hall and informing passersby about the "kangaroo court" he just left. Gremillion had received a sixty-day suspended jail sentence on a criminal contempt charge, and it seemed as he stood before the U.S. Supreme Court justifying his prosecution of Garrison on similar grounds that the justices were resurrecting the incident. In an attempt to change the subject, Gremillion reminded the court twice more that Garrison had not taken the stand in his own defense. It appeared an empty gesture. As the hearing ended, the justices seemed more interested in Jack Gremillion than Jim Garrison.[31]

Two days after oral arguments, with the public portion of their deliberative process completed, the court's members entered their oak-paneled conference room to discuss the week's cases. The weekly conference began as it had since Reconstruction—the justices filed into the book-lined room, shook hands amicably, and then took their seats around the rectangular table. The justices were the only people allowed in the room during the weekly conference, and they stressed the strictest secrecy. Only Justice Douglas's handwritten notes provide a glimpse into the conclave. Most justices took notes during conferences, but in order to maintain the meeting's cherished secrecy, some ordered the notes destroyed upon their deaths. Fortunately, Douglas's concise notes remain, and they portray a court divided as to what merit Garrison's appeal had—if any. For instance, although the chief justice did not believe Garrison's statements contained actual malice as defined in the *Times* decision, he expressed greater concern that Louisiana law denied the appellant a jury trial even in the face of a one-year jail term. Not surprisingly, Douglas and Black, without comment, voted to reverse the conviction; both men had expressed in the *Times* case and in other decisions a shared belief that the First Amendment forbade even the existence of libel laws. Like Warren, Douglas, and Black, Brennan also believed the court should upend Garrison's conviction, but for reasons to which he had alluded during oral arguments—that the court should use the case to apply the actual malice standard to criminal libel cases as it had to civil libel in the *Times* decision. "Criminal libel as applied to public officials is unconstitutional," Douglas quoted Brennan, adding that the "*Times* [decision] was civil libel, [but] there is no room here at all for criminal libel." Unaccountably, Brennan made a bolder assertion in the coming days as the court's internal deliberations continued. He abandoned the idea of extending the *Times* rule to incorporate criminal as well as civil libel cases and instead moved to strike down state criminal defamation statutes all together. Brennan's radical stance caused major dissension among the court's more moderate members and doomed his attempts to reach a consensus during the current term.[32]

The fracture among the justices grew as the discussion continued around the table. Goldberg, who in his second year on the court was quickly becoming an entrenched liberal, took an oddly moderate position. Garrison's statements appeared malicious to Goldberg, but, like Warren, he believed no law stripped a defendant of his right to a jury trial. Justices Clark and Harlan, the court's consistently conservative members, both supported Garrison's conviction. Harlan, notable for his belief that federal courts should limit their interference in state matters, believed that any action by the Supreme Court to restrain a state's ability to prosecute criminal libel actions was dangerous. He further insisted the court did not have enough evidence either of malice or of Garrison's innocence to reverse the case. To Clark, however, it was clear Garrison had intended to defame the New Orleans judges. "He talked at length, showing the extreme nature of his comments," Douglas quoted Clark, who added that there was "plenty of evidence of malice here." Justice Stewart favored remanding the case back to the state court to be retried under the *Times* actual malice standard. The final court member, Justice White, passed without comment when his turn came. With discussion concluded, the chief justice conducted an official vote. Five justices, Warren, Black, Douglas, Brennan, and Goldberg, indicated their desire to reverse Garrison's conviction, but for disparate reasons. As expected, Harlan and Clark voted to affirm the decision. Stewart still favored remanding the case to the state court for retrial under the actual malice rule, while White indicated no preference. The conference ended with the court decidedly fractured and with no definite mandate as to what would become of Garrison's appeal.[33]

As the majority's ranking member, the chief justice selected who he wanted to write the court's opinion. Warren chose Brennan, to whom he also had delegated drafting the *Times* ruling. It was a wise move on Warren's part, given the fissured nature of the court's attitude toward Garrison's case. In his eight years on the court, Brennan had emerged as Warren's chief lieutenant and confidant, but moreover he had gained a reputation as a consensus-builder. Although five justices had voted to overturn Garrison's conviction, their continued support was far from guaranteed. If Brennan failed to draft an opinion acceptable to each of the justices, some might decide to write opinions of their own. With only a five-person majority, the loss of any justice would result in the lack of a court mandate, essentially a legal deadend for Garrison's case and the questions it raised.[34]

Brennan undoubtedly strove to avoid such an outcome, but the first draft opinion he circulated on May 16, 1964, only deepened the court's division. During oral arguments, Brennan had asserted the possibility that the court might extend the *Times* standard to include criminal as well as civil libel suits. For reasons that remain unclear,

however, Brennan's first draft barely mentioned his earlier suggestion. Instead, the justice took a defiantly more radical approach that
struck down all state criminal libel laws. Such statutes, he contended,
allowed for the possibility of sedition prosecutions. Using Louisiana
as an example, Brennan contended that the state had applied its defamation statute as a sedition law. He insisted that the state's statute
intended not to protect individuals' rights of free expression, but to
suppress criticism of government action. He characterized such use
as "impermissible . . . Government is not then acting the role of impartial umpire and its use of the criminal process must therefore be
held as offensive" to the First Amendment and its free speech guarantees. Such libel prosecutions, Brennan continued, have "no place
in the American system of jurisprudence." With that, the Supreme
Court would have obliterated state criminal libel laws. Had a majority
of the court's members endorsed the opinion, the results of *Garrison
v. Louisiana* would have surpassed the *Times* ruling in unshackling
free speech rights in the United States. It was not to be, and Brennan's
sweeping opinion only widened the philosophical chasm within the
court.[35]

Brennan's draft drew disparate and passionate reactions from
the other justices. Without comment, Chief Justice Warren joined,
or signaled his unconditional approval for the opinion. Justice Stewart, who had favored remanding the case back to the state courts for
a retrial under the *Times* actual malice standard, sent Brennan a brief
memorandum on May 19 that noted his support but indicated his continued hesitation. "It is conceivable that a dissent could dislodge me,"
Stewart wrote, "but as of now I am with you." With three votes for his
majority opinion, including his, Brennan awaited the six remaining
justices' reactions.[36]

Not surprisingly, Justice Clark, who in conference had voted to
uphold Garrison's conviction, told his fellow justices on May 20 he
would issue a dissent. Eight days later, Clark circulated his first draft
in which he vehemently rejected Brennan's seditious libel approach.
In the draft's opening pages, Clark referred to the argument as "a
straw dragon" and dismissed the premise that the Supreme Court
should limit a state's ability to prosecute criminal defamation cases.
He further insisted that libel incited crimes and other breaches of the

peace, echoing an argument Assistant Attorney General Michael E. Culligan had asserted in his initial brief on behalf of the state of Louisiana. Furthermore, Clark implicitly stated his belief that Garrison— whom he referred to as "Morrison" throughout the early draft—unquestionably intended to injure the judges' private reputations with his comments. The mere fact that the judges were public officials and not private citizens "does not change the defamation to seditious libel," Clark insisted. Garrison's comments "were purely epithets of personal abuse with no essential value . . . pure and simple falsehood, maliciously made, to defame the character, reputation, and personal integrity" of the judges. In this case, Louisiana did not apply its defamation statute to suppress criticism, but rather to ensure "the public peace" and to protect "the personal reputation of eight of its citizens from false charges, maliciously made, of their personal criminality." Clark ended his dissent by noting with regret that by striking down state criminal defamation laws, the court removed any responsibility from individuals, who might now use the ruling as a shield to defame with impunity. "This is a dangerous doctrine, foreign to our history, and it will encourage and make bolder those who make use of false charges of criminality to defame the respectability of public officers," Clark concluded, adding: "Indeed, today's decision may be but a flag to hate-mongers to pour even more venom into our public bloodstream." Clark's impassioned dissent further threatened any chance to secure a court majority.[37]

Other justices, uncomfortable with the radical tenor of Brennan's opinion, moved to join Clark's dissent. On June 1, Justice Harlan, who like Clark had voted to affirm Garrison's conviction, added his name to Clark's dissent. Harlan suggested that Clark tone down some of the draft's most colorful phrases; when Clark again circulated his dissent on June 2, he had removed the "straw dragon" characterization, as well as an allegation that Brennan's opinion had used the Sedition Act of 1798 as a "whipping boy" to justify the *Garrison* decision.[38]

Brennan, clearly attempting to salvage a majority and to answer Clark's dissenting opinion, issued a third draft on June 2.[39] The new draft further demonstrated the central obstruction the court faced in reaching a consensus—it could not agree if Garrison's statements concerned the judges' private character or their public reputations. Although Clark insisted Garrison's comments hit at the judges' private lives, Brennan simply could not concede—even for the sake of a court consensus—that the justices could protect a public official's private life from criticism. "Any criticism of the manner in which a public official goes about his duties will tend to affect his private reputation," the justice concluded, but Brennan's insistence did little to dislodge the ever-growing discontent among the court's other members.[40]

An incongruity between the *Times* decision and the *Garrison* opinion further divided the justices. Brennan's first *Garrison* draft noted that the *Times* actual malice standard had provided state governments with a criterion by which they could measure civil libel. "What is true of a civil libel law is also true of a criminal libel law," Brennan wrote, but in the remainder of his opinion, the justice never said explicitly that the actual malice standard should apply to criminal libel cases. Instead, he focused on the seditious libel approach that would bar states from prosecuting criminal libel cases all together. Several court members pointed out the conflict between the *Times* ruling, which had provided a malice test for civil libel, and the *Garrison* majority decision, which offered no such standard for criminal cases. Justice Douglas, in a concurring opinion issued on June 2, first noted the contradiction.[41] He quoted Brennan's draft and asked rhetorically, "How can we say in [the *Garrison*] case that the 'Constitution flatly bars criminal prosecutions based on the mere criticism of public men for their private conduct' and yet find no controlling difference in other libel suits where 'actual malice' is present?" The refusal to extend a standard to criminal libel was not Douglas's sole disagreement with the *Garrison* decision. He also wanted the court to strike down all libel laws, whether criminal or civil, a view he expressed in a concurring opinion in the *Times* case. The malice standard, he repeated in his *Garrison* opinion, was flawed, and the *Times* definition of malice was difficult to prove. Malice, he suggested, was always present in the "heat and passion" of public debate, and the court should not restrict the intensity of public discourse by allowing libel laws to continue. The court's ruling was "pale and tame," Douglas wrote, concluding the libel laws and free speech were simply contradictory.[42]

In a third draft on June 4, Justice Clark noted his agreement with Douglas—it was inconsistent to establish a standard for one set of libel laws but not to do the same for the other. Clark made clear that although he and Douglas agreed on this point, it was only on this point. He could not support unrestricted freedom of speech. Neither could Justice White, who issued a dissent on June 10. White's dissent provided a primer on the incongruity between the *Times* decision and the *Garrison* case. Like Douglas and Clark, White argued that the *Garrison* decision was inconsistent with the *Times* ruling and, in striking down all state criminal libel statutes, the court "lumps the known lie in with honest criticism and extends to both the cloak of constitutional immunity." White maintained that the *Times* decision had eliminated First Amendment protection for calculated falsehood in civil actions, but by striking down all state criminal libel laws, the court left no possibility for individuals—either private citizens or public officials—to seek criminal damages. "It is therefore difficult to understand how the author of a lie should have his First Amendment defense overruled in a civil action but sustained by the same court in a criminal proceeding," White argued. The *Times* decision had sustained the possibility of civil libel action by establishing the actual malice standard; a public official could recover civil damages if he proved his accuser had impugned his reputation with knowledge of a statement's falsity or with disregard to whether the statement was false or not. White maintained that Brennan's *Garrison* opinion did not follow the example set in the *Times* case. Brennan had irrationally struck down all state criminal libel actions without providing an applicable standard by which courts could measure potentially libelous utterances, White concluded.[43]

Despite his objections to the majority opinion, White agreed that the court should reverse Garrison's conviction, but only because the justice did not believe the standard by which the Louisiana court had measured Garrison's statements was constitutionally sound. Under the Louisiana defamation statute, a court could find a person guilty of defamation simply by proving that malice motivated his comments; truth was no defense under Louisiana law. This standard was irreconcilable with the *Times* decision, White wrote. He then suggested that the Supreme Court remand Garrison's case to the state level, where he could be retried using the *Times* actual malice standard. If the court struck down criminal libel laws, it risked "immunizing falsehood" by granting First Amendment protection to malicious liars and libelers, White insisted. By providing the states with a reasoned alternative to prosecute criminal libel, the court could balance the right of free speech with the rights of states to protect their citizens.[44]

Many of White's suggestions would resurface in the court's eventual *Garrison* opinion, released during its next session. As the current term rapidly concluded, however, a consensus appeared increasingly unlikely. As of June 10, when White issued his dissent, only three justices—Brennan, Warren, and Stewart—had joined the majority opinion. Douglas had issued a concurring opinion, which Black had joined on June 11. Justice Goldberg also had penned a concurrence, in which he largely reiterated the arguments he had made in a concurring opinion in the *Times* case. Finally, justices Clark and Harlan had affixed their names to a dissent. With the court fragmented, Harlan began to hear talk from his clerks and the other justices that White's decision could very well become the majority opinion. Stewart, for one, was thinking about abandoning Brennan's opinion. Clark's clerk suggested the justice scrap his dissent and join White's opinion. Harlan, however, expressed doubts about White's position and urged Clark to address those concerns in their joint dissent. White suggested that Louisiana's standard of malice, which allowed defamation prosecutions regardless if a speaker's words were true or not, was constitutionally unsound; he had also argued that Garrison should be retried on the state level using the *Times* actual malice test. To Harlan, an impassioned believer in federalism and the autonomy of states, the *Times* test was less stringent than Louisiana's statute. White's position "would hold invalid a more rigorous standard than one which it believes valid," Harlan wrote to Clark, who included his colleague's sentiments in a draft opinion he circulated on June 15.[45]

As the court neared summer recess, it appeared that a resolution was unlikely. Technically, the court could have issued the opinions as they stood, but unanimity had long been an important factor among the Warren Court justices. To release several conflicting opinions would only confuse the situation, offer little interpretive assistance to the lower courts, and provide no clear conclusion to Garrison's appeal. On June 22, 1964, the last day of the October 1963 term, the

court, without comment, restored the case to its calendar for reargu-
ment during its next session.[46] A combination of factors doomed the Supreme Court's attempts
to secure a majority opinion. Garrison's appeal required the court to
consider for the first time whether a state could use a defamation statute to curtail criticism of public officials. That question alone guaranteed no easy solution for the justices, but other issues contributed to
the court's disharmony. The dissonance centered on the incongruity
between the court's *Times* opinion, which offered a standard to judge
civil libel suits, and Brennan's *Garrison* opinion, which set no such
guidelines for criminal libel. Brennan's radical approach eliminating
all state criminal defamation statutes alienated the more moderate
justices like White and Stewart and failed to gain even the support
of ardent First Amendment advocates like Black, Douglas, and Goldberg. Brennan's sweeping opinion also guaranteed the opposition of
Clark and Harlan, the court's most conservative members, who consistently pointed out yet another problem with Garrison's appeal—its
malevolent origins. In the next term, the court continued to grapple
with the restrictions state criminal defamation laws placed on free
speech as well as the *Garrison* case's troubling genesis. Only through
oral arguments, further deliberations, and Brennan's consensus-
building efforts would the court reach an accord and release an opinion that solidified Jim Garrison's political influence in New Orleans.
More important, the Supreme Court's ruling in *Garrison v. Louisiana*
would finally transform what had been a feud over money and power
into a landmark decision that expanded the fundamental right of free
speech in the United States.

CHAPTER V

From Self-Doubt to "the Essence of Self-Government":
The Supreme Court Salvages *Garrison v. Louisiana*

A rectangular sheet of white butcher paper symbolized Earl Warren's control of the U.S. Supreme Court. As chief justice, Warren was *primus inter pares*, first among equals, and his duties were largely the same as those the court's other members shouldered—with one notable exception. During the court's weekly conference, Warren kept a tabulation of the justices' votes as they decided what cases to hear or how the court would rule on accepted petitions. If Warren voted with the majority, he secured the right to select which justice would write the court's opinion. By assigning the majority cases, Warren effectively controlled the court's decision-making process and, in a larger sense, the entire federal judicial system. After each conference, the chief justice retreated to his own chambers, pulled out the assignment chart he kept on the large sheet of plain white stock, and determined what justice would receive which case. It was perhaps the most political act of the court's ostensibly nonpartisan operations.[1]

On June 22, 1964, Warren studied the assignment chart. Across the top of the sheet was each justices' name, under which were listed the cases each of the court's members were assigned. Under the name of Associate Justice William J. Brennan, Warren neatly crossed through number four hundred, *Garrison v. Louisiana*, and noted the case was "to be reargued" when the court resumed after the summer recess. Since the previous spring, when it first heard oral arguments in the case, the court had grappled with Orleans Parish District Attorney Jim Garrison's appeal and had attempted to determine how it could reconcile constitutionally the existence of state defamation laws with the First Amendment's free speech protections. The justices drafted hundreds of pages in their quest for a consensus, but common ground had eluded them. When the rehearing of *Garrison v. Louisiana* commenced two weeks into the October 1964 term, it quickly became apparent what the court hoped to accomplish with the proceedings. Unknown to anyone but the justices themselves, the court wanted the litigants' counsel to remove the uncertainty of the previous spring's deliberations and resolve the court's own internal arguments. As a result, the second round of oral arguments tested the attorneys' legal prowess. One lawyer realized that the Supreme Court had elevated the case beyond its genesis as a provincial political fight; the other seemed unable to comprehend that he was no longer prosecuting a defendant but rather attempting to uphold Louisiana's criminal defamation law. The question at the center of Garrison's appeal was not one of guilt or innocence, but rather of the constitutionality of the statute under which the state had prosecuted him. The attorneys' ability to recognize that distinction determined the case's outcome and laid the foundation for a significant expansion of First Amendment rights in the United States.[2]

The court scheduled the rehearing for *Garrison v. Louisiana*, now number four on the docket, on October 19, 1964. Again, Eberhard P. Deutsch defended Garrison, while Attorney General Jack P.F. Gremillion represented the state of Louisiana. Deutsch commenced his presentation by updating the justices as to the improved jail situation in Orleans Parish, the increased judicial work hours, and the renewed relationship between the judges and District Attorney Garrison. However, one situation had not improved, Deutsch told the justices. The state continued to employ its criminal defamation statute to suppress criticism. Only twelve days before, on October 7, 1964, the Louisiana Supreme Court had denied a rehearing for an African-American minister, B. Elton Cox, whom police in Baton Rouge had arrested for breach of peace after he had led a civil rights demonstration in front of the parish courthouse. After his arrest, Cox accused a parish judge and the district attorney of accepting bribes. Officials charged him with violating the same criminal defamation statute under which the state had prosecuted Garrison. An East Baton Rouge Parish court found Cox guilty on two counts of defamation and leveled a total fine of $6,000 and a two-year jail sentence.[3] Cox's plight, Deutsch told the justices, "demonstrates the frightful use to which a statute of this sort can be used . . . Our position is simply that when a statute of this sort is used to support seditious libel [prosecutions], it is invalid" under the First Amendment. The justices then began to question Deutsch. Some justices believed that Brennan's opinion the previous term, which had deemed all state defamation laws unconstitutional, left public officials' private lives vulnerable to criticism. It was a major point of contention that doomed Brennan's efforts to garner a majority. During reargument, Brennan now posed a hypothetical situation to Deutsch to gauge the lawyer's opinion as to whether the court could separate an official's public character and his private life. The justice's question also exposed the court's internal struggle the previous term. Brennan asked:

> Brennan: What is your definition of seditious libel?
> Deutsch: Putting it very succinctly, defamation of a government official, a public official.
> Brennan: Even in his personal capacity?
> Deutsch: Perhaps not, but it's almost impossible to separate the two.
> Brennan: What if you said in the same breath: 'He's a very fine judge, but he's a notorious adulterer?'
> Deutsch: Well, I would take it that adultery is not a characteristic of judges and accordingly would refer to his personal rather than his judicial capacity. By and large, I think there is a distinction, but there is a very broad shadow zone. It's awfully hard to say that a judge is under racketeering influence and then say in the same breath that it does not refer to his official capacity. I can't conceive of that.[4]

Deutsch had no way of knowing it, but with these questions, Brennan sought the lawyer's help in convincing his colleagues of the impossibility of separating an official's private life from his public duties. In search of a clear mandate, Brennan was willing to concede and compromise only so much—he truly believed that it was futile for the court to delineate between the two spheres of an official's life.[5]

Taking Brennan's lead, another justice asked Deutsch if public officials enjoyed any First Amendment safeguards from criticism. Yes, Deutsch replied, but not in their official capacities. Then the justice engaged in another hypothetical, the second in less than twenty minutes. What if, the justice asked, someone said a public official "cheats on the golf course, that he cheats his friends every Saturday when he plays golf?" Deutsch responded, to the laughter of the crowd and the justices:

Well, again, you are within that shadow zone because a
man who would do that isn't fit to hold public office! The
shadow zone is so broad to me that there is almost no way
to separate his personal character from his public character. If he has a bad personal character, he is not fit to serve
the public. . . . When you speak in realities as we are in
this case, stating that a judge is subject to racketeer influence . . . a *judge* is subject . . . you are not saying John Doe
. . . you are not even in the shadow zone. That's clearly in
his capacity as a public official.[6]

As Brennan had done earlier, the justice here suggested that the court
would be unable to protect a public official's private life from criticism.[7]

Not all of the court's members were convinced, however. Justice
Byron R. White, whose dissenting opinion the previous term had expressed a fear that the court was offering liars the protection of the
First Amendment, tried to dissect Deutsch's—though really Brennan's—seditious libel argument. White posed yet another theoreti-
cal situation. An individual criticizes a public official using a known
lie "for the express purpose of destroying a man's reputation," White
hypothesized before asking, "Why shouldn't this fellow be open to
criminal prosecution? Your only answer so far has been a label [sedi-
tious libel]." Deutsch responded that lies were, like it or not, a part
of public life and that the First Amendment protected all speech re-
lating to public affairs. "So," White responded, "to protect the truth,
we should protect the lie also?" Deutsch answered affirmatively, not
knowing that White's opinion the previous term had expressed his belief that lies undermined the First Amendment and deserved no constitutional protection. Justice Hugo L. Black, knowing this to be the
case, came to Deutsch's aid and again expressed his position that government had no right to limit free speech in any manner. "You mean,
Mr. Deutsch, that it's the old notion if you can't stand the heat, stay
out of the kitchen?" Black asked, chuckling. The attorney responded:
"Exactly. I think that's a part of public life in a democracy, and I think
it's a good thing that it is." Despite Black's assertion, however, White
remained unconvinced. He continued to worry that the actual malice

Jim Garrison, the "Battling District Attorney," poses on Bourbon Street, May 1963.

The five nightclubs closed as a result of December 1, 1962, raids: El Morocco (above); Club Sultana (below); Guys and Dolls (opposite, top); Jazz, Ltd. (opposite, middle); Club Flamingo (opposite, bottom).

BOURBON STREET ASSOCIATION OF NIGHT CLUBS

522 RUE BOURBON   NEW ORLEANS 16, LA.

FOR IMMEDIATE RELEASE   (September 24, 1962)

The officers and members of the Bourbon Street Association of Night Clubs have instructed me to issue the following statement on their behalf:

"Notwithstanding the 'unofficial' statement of a representative of the District Attorney's Office, the decision to close Bourbon Street Clubs had nothing whatever to do with arrests made last Friday. It is absurd for anyone to state that 12 Clubs closed simply because isolated instances of police action took place in two of them.

"It is true that the so-called vice drive of the District Attorney has degenerated into a sporadic campaign of harassment in which arrests for everything but vice violations have been made. Club Owners have been repeatedly molested by police agents screaming about doors being open, doors being closed, lights being too dim, patrons being too boisterous, employees using profane language, etc. This has been the extent of the highly advertised clean-up campaign which the District Attorney has pursued with such vigor.

"One part of the reason for closing is that Club Owners had gone to considerable expense and trouble to establish a system whereby undesirable personnel and illicit activities would be eliminated entirely from the operation of Bourbon Street Clubs. However, it has been demonstrated to the Owners that some officials are not really interested in having a well-regulated and well-behaved Bourbon Street, but rather are interested in using the Street to create the image of themselves as champions of justice and moral purity. The Club Owners do not feel that they can afford to continue to be made the goat for these ambitious politicians and will not reopen until they feel they can earn a living without being subjected to the whims of irresponsible persons in authority.

"The Club Owners wish to make it clear that they have neither resented nor resisted any program to rid Bourbon Street of undesirable persons and practices and that they do not now ask for or expect any preferential treatment. Further, they wish to go on record as wholeheartedly endorsing any effort to jail and convict law violators, but thus far their attempts to help New Orleans by helping themselves have met only official indifference and even derision. They except the Commission Council which at least gave them a hearing and granted their request to attend to one facet of their intended program.

"They have proposed to invest thousands of dollars in a promotional program to make Bourbon Street the nation's capital of adult entertainment, but if New Orleans is not interested in giving them a chance to put this program into effect, they have no choice but to consider remaining closed permanently. Certainly they have no intention of reopening within 72 hours contrary to the prediction of uninformed persons."

Hubert Badeaux
Public Relations Director

A public relations letter sent out in the Fall of 1962 on behalf of Bourbon Street clubs, which questioned the motives of the Garrison-led crackdown on vice.

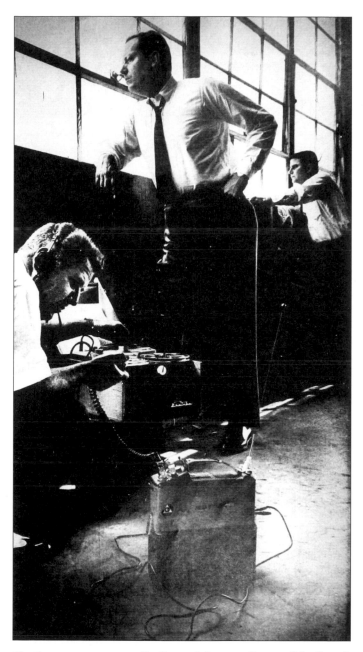

Garrison, center, personally directed the surveillance of the French Quarter nightclubs. Chief Investigator Pershing O. Gervais is at left.

The eight judges of the Orleans Parish Criminal District Court (left to right) Bernard J. Bagert, Sr., Malcolm V. O'Hara, Shirley Wimberly, Oliver Schulingkamp (obscured), George W. Platt, Thomas M. Brahney, Jr., Edward A. Haggerty, Jr., and J. Bernard Cocke.

The U.S. Supreme Court in 1963: (standing, left to right) Byron White, William Brennan, Potter Stewart, Arthur Goldberg, (seated, left to right) Tom Clark, Hugo Black, Earl Warren, William Douglas, and John Marshall Harlan.

Louisiana Attorney General Jack P. F. Gremillion's inept performance was critical in the U.S. Supreme Court's overturning Garrison's defamation conviction.

"The Last Madam," Norma Wallace, who said of Garrison's raids "I've seen D.A.s become ex-D.A.s, and police chiefs become ex-police chiefs, and mayors become ex-mayors. But I've never become an ex-madam."

Jim Garrison later received worldwide attention for his investigation of the assassination of President John F. Kennedy. His failed conspiracy prosecution of New Orleans businessman Clay L. Shaw remains the only public trial in the Kennedy case.

standard would offer First Amendment protection to lies as well as the truth.[8]

If the justices were looking to Louisiana Attorney General Jack Gremillion to help them sort out their disagreements, they were disappointed. In discussing the importance of oral arguments, Justice John Marshall Harlan II once explained that the court voted on cases usually within days of oral presentations. As a result, the arguments remained fresh in the justices' minds and often proved decisive. Based on their exchanges with the ill-prepared and often-befuddled attorney general and from comments during their later conference, the justices were unimpressed with Gremillion's presentation of the state's case. As in the earlier oral arguments, it often seemed that Gremillion— not Garrison—was the subject of the court's deliberations, especially when the justices discovered that the attorney general could not recall key passages of the defamation law he was defending.[9] The Louisiana statute punished any malicious statement, whether true or false. Although the definition of malice was in obvious disagreement with the standard the Supreme Court established in *New York Times v. Sullivan*, Gremillion argued passionately that the two were indeed harmonious. Obviously ill at ease, he interrupted justices—a major etiquette breach under the court's rules—and persisted to the point where a justice admonished him for his behavior. When another justice asked about Louisiana's malice standard and how it differed from the *Times* decision, Gremillion replied that the prosecution had proven malice during the lower court proceedings. The justices, including Brennan, repeatedly asked the attorney general to provide evidence of malice as the court had defined it in *Times*. Gremillion could not and told the court:

> Gremillion: The record shows actual malice . . . we proved about the vacations, we proved about the vice, we put the chief of police of the city of New Orleans on [the stand], we put the judges on, we actually put the vouchers in . . .
>
> Brennan: You proved [Garrison's] statements were false?
>
> Gremillion: We proved the statements were false and we proved they were made with malice.

> Brennan: Where is the evidence of malice? I agree
> with you that there is evidence as to whether the state-
> ments were true or false, but what about the malice?[10]

When Gremillion again referred the justices to pages in the record
of the lower court proceedings, it became apparent to the court that
the Louisiana attorney general could not define the actual malice
standard the court had set forth in *Times*. One justice kindly supplied
Gremillion with the definition, but the attorney general by then was
so perplexed that when the justice repeated his request for evidence
of actual malice on Garrison's part, he again pointed to the record,
where he said the justices could find "about ten pages devoted to malice." Gremillion was unable to comprehend that he was no longer
prosecuting Garrison, but rather defending Louisiana's defamation
law. The attorney general's embarrassing lack of preparation resur-
faced repeatedly and doomed his efforts to uphold Garrison's conviction and to demonstrate the constitutionality of the state's statute.[11]

As Gremillion's half-hour presentation mercifully neared its conclusion, a question from Chief Justice Warren again revealed the attorney general's uncertainty about a contentious portion of the Louisiana defamation statute—the provision that made truth no defense
in a criminal libel proceeding. In response to Warren's question, Gremillion denied ever telling the court that the statute made malicious
statements, whether true or false, punishable. "You have answered
'yes' to that question at least six times," during the course of the proceeding, Justice White snapped, before providing Gremillion with a
page number in *Deutsch's* brief where he might find Louisiana's definition of malice. The attorney general still appeared confused, and a
final hypothetical from Warren further bewildered him. Under the
chief justice's scenario, a judge solicited a bribe from a litigant in a case
before his court. The man, so outraged at the behavior, made public
the solicitation. Could Louisiana prosecute that man for telling the
truth? Warren asked. Gremillion said yes, but recanted, insisting,
"No, I don't think he could be prosecuted under that set of circumstances. He would have a complete defense . . . of the truth." Warren
then reminded Gremillion that Louisiana's statute made truth no
defense. The attorney general, obviously exhausted, sighed and then

insisted that he was arguing the case "the way it is." After a few more comments, Gremillion returned to his seat.[12]

With Gremillion's performance fresh in their minds, the justices gathered for the weekly conference on October 23, four days after rehearing Garrison's appeal. The chief justice began the discussion, and then each justice spoke in order of seniority. They quickly reached at least one consensus—Gremillion had not proven that the Louisiana defamation statute should stand. Five of nine justices said the statute was void "on its face," which meant Garrison's conviction deserved a reversal simply because the state had presented no persuasive evidence to the contrary. The justices then discussed how to proceed. The court could reverse Garrison's conviction as it simultaneously struck down the defamation statute as disharmonious with the *Times* actual malice standard. However, several justices saw the *Garrison* case as a chance to clear up ambiguity in its *Times* decision and to extend the case's protections against civil libel to criminal libel as well. Warren, White, Tom C. Clark, Potter Stewart, and Arthur J. Goldberg Jr. suggested applying the actual malice standard to criminal libel, thereby limiting an official's right to seek damages through either civil or criminal libel suits. Clark and Harlan wanted to remand the case to the state court for a new trial under the *Times* actual malice rule; their proposition led to a debate on whether Garrison's statements would pass such a test. Douglas said his remarks would not, because there was too much evidence of malice on Garrison's part. He favored overturning the conviction simply because he believed the statute allowed sedition prosecutions. As he had when the justices first discussed the case in April, Clark asserted his belief that it was not a sedition prosecution at all, but rather one for personal defamation. He repeated his contention that Garrison's statements indeed were defamatory and if the court remanded the case to the state level, Garrison would likely be found guilty under the *Times* actual malice standard. Harlan agreed with Clark that applying the seditious libel label to the prosecution was an overstatement and agreed that Garrison's remarks did not meet the test established in *Times*. Like Clark, he also favored a new trial, but the other justices argued that they could use Garrison's appeal to clarify and enhance the earlier *Times* decision.[13]

After the discussion concluded, Warren conducted the vote. Eight justices favored overturning the conviction, while Clark, as he had the previous term, still disagreed. Warren again selected Brennan to write the opinion of the court. From the time the chief justice assigned the case to him on October 27, it became Brennan's task to unite the court behind a single, unambiguous decision. Despite the eight to one reversal, the justices could disagree on specific points in Brennan's draft and even switch their votes to dissent outright. Wanting to avoid the opposition his opinions had generated during the previous term and eager to convey a unified statement that reaffirmed his *Times* decision, Brennan abandoned his earlier seditious libel approach to overturning Garrison's conviction.[14]

Between November 14 and November 21, 1964, Brennan circulated among the justices five draft opinions, none of which mentioned the word "sedition." Instead, he followed the lead of five of his fellow justices—Warren, Goldberg, Stewart, White, and Clark—all of whom had expressed their desire during the conference discussion to extend the *Times* actual malice standard to include criminal as well as civil libel cases. In unambiguous language, Brennan did just that, holding: "At the outset, we must decide whether, in view of the differing history and purposes of criminal libel, the *New York Times* rule also limits state power to impose criminal sanctions for criticism of the official conduct of public officials. We hold that it does." The court, Brennan continued, did not find any distinction between criminal libel statutes and civil libel laws "where criticism of public officials is concerned." The broad Louisiana statute, which allowed no defense of the truth and punished even criticism based on fact, posed a hazard to free speech, Brennan wrote. "Debate on public issues will not be uninhibited if the speaker must run the risk that it will be proved in court that he spoke out of hatred; indeed, even utterances motivated by hatred, so long as they are honestly believed, contribute to the free exchange of ideas and the ascertainment of the truth," the justice suggested. Therefore, a state could only punish erroneous statements if the speaker had "a high degree of awareness" as to the falsity of his claims. The First Amendment demanded protection for unpopular and even controversial speech, even when based on mistaken information, because such debate furthered public discourse,

Brennan insisted. "For speech concerning public affairs is more than self-expression," he wrote, "it is the essence of self-government." It would become the opinion's most-quoted phrase because it concisely stated the importance Garrison's case had assumed. What had begun on Bourbon Street as a struggle over money and power now emerged as an unambiguous statement of the right of Americans to criticize public leaders. In one sentence, Brennan endowed dissent with the protection of the U.S. Constitution.[15]

In the draft's opening pages, Brennan clearly attempted to appeal to justices who had dissented during the court's discussion of the case the previous term. Brennan hoped his new, more moderate opinion and the attorneys' performance during the second round of oral arguments had altered his colleagues' earlier views. Justices Clark and White had disagreed with Brennan's initial opinion that had upended all state criminal libel statutes. They feared Brennan's opinion offered constitutional protection to deliberate lies and limited a state's ability to prosecute purveyors of inflammatory speech. During oral arguments in October, White asked Deutsch if he believed the Constitution protected lies as well as the truth; Deutsch answered affirmatively, not knowing of White's own stance. Now, attempting to bring White and Clark firmly into the majority, Brennan incorporated their ideas into the new opinion. The First Amendment did not protect deliberate lies, even when they concerned public affairs, Brennan now contended. Calculated falsehoods, he wrote, were "at odds with the premises of democratic government," and rightly lost immunity from prosecution. In his search for a consensus, Brennan refused to ascribe to the view Deutsch espoused during oral arguments—that in order to protect the truth, the First Amendment must protect lies as well. The justice had already described criticism as "the essence of self-government," and he would not sully the sanctity of the fundamental right to dissent by granting lies the same constitutional protection. In addition, Brennan knew that a strong statement dismissing falsehoods as antidemocratic would win the support of White and Clark and help guarantee a majority.[16]

During conference discussion, the justices had divided over whether Garrison's statements were indeed true and whether a lower court, using the *Times* actual malice doctrine, would again convict him if retried. In his continued effort to form a consensus, Brennan decided the court should not address the validity of Garrison's criticisms against the judges. Instead, he wrote that the district attorney had admonished the judges' official duties, not their private reputations as the lower courts had held. Despite his desire for unanimity, however, Brennan would not abandon an argument he espoused the previous term—that criticism of an official's public duties would affect his private life. Indeed, it would be impossible for the court to separate the two, and Brennan again suggested that "any criticism of the manner in which a public official performs his duties" affected both his private and public reputations. "To this end," the justice insisted, "anything which might touch on an official's fitness for office is relevant," including accusations of dishonesty in his private dealings. The public's right to know about their elected officials outweighed any interest an officeholder may have in protecting his private reputation, Brennan concluded. In short, an official could no longer delineate between his private life and his public duties; one invariably affected the other. Brennan's conclusion greatly broadened the right of individuals to criticize all facets of an official's life, while it simultaneously limited an officeholder's ability to retaliate through criminal defamation proceedings.[17]

By November 18, four days after circulating his opinion's first draft, Brennan had received only one notice of support—from the chief justice. Justice Clark told his clerk he wanted to gauge Justice White's feelings before either joining the majority or sticking with his dissenting vote. Justices Goldberg and William O. Douglas intended to write separate, concurring opinions. Justice Black joined Douglas' opinion and later issued a concurrence of his own. As Brennan circulated the third draft of his opinion, the harmony he wanted continued to elude him, and the choice of language in this draft only complicated matters.[18] In Brennan's first draft, he wrote that Louisiana could not retry Garrison "under the statute," meaning that the state, if it chose to retry Garrison, could only do so under a revised law that incorporated the *Times* actual malice test. In the third draft, however, Brennan shifted some words and implied that Louisiana could not retry Garrison at all, even if it rewrote its defamation law. Not only did this change threaten Brennan's majority, but it also would invariably result in intense debate and scrutiny by legal scholars, lawyers, judges, and the public. Brennan knew that to avoid both situations, he would have to compromise, and the next day, November 19, Brennan circulated a fourth draft with a memorandum to Clark, Harlan, Stewart, and White attached. Those four justices, at one time or another throughout discussion of the *Garrison* case, had favored remanding the case to the lower courts to decide under the *Times* malice standard. His draft the previous day had left no room for any state action. In the memorandum, he offered a compromise—he would not mention a retrial at all "so as to leave it to [Louisiana] to figure out, without instruction from us, whether or not to try Garrison again." It worked. Later that same day, all four justices sent Brennan notes that indicated their desire to join his opinion. Brennan, ever the consensus builder, finally had his majority.[19]

Discontent remained in Justice Douglas' chambers, however, and it threatened the court's cohesion. Douglas remained firm in the conviction he had expressed when the court heard the *Garrison* case the previous term—the Louisiana defamation law was the very essence of a sedition statute. That alone did not pose a threat to the court's public unity, but Douglas' contention that Garrison intentionally defamed the Orleans Parish judges did. In a draft opinion he shared on November 18 with Justice Black, a fellow First Amendment absolutist, Douglas agreed that the Louisiana statute should be overturned and Garrison's conviction reversed, not because the lower courts had failed to demonstrate malice but because he believed all criminal libel laws violated free speech. The court's *Garrison* ruling did not go far enough to protect the First Amendment, Douglas opined, nor did the *Times* rule provide an adequate barometer to test malicious statements. Nevertheless, as the rule stood, Douglas insisted he "would have great difficulty concluding" a court would not find that malice had actuated Garrison's statements. When Black returned the draft to Douglas, he bracketed the explicit sentence and wrote next to it that some might construe the statement to indicate the court's belief that Garrison was guilty.[20]

The sentence did not appear in subsequent drafts, but Douglas continued to believe that Garrison was guilty. Earlier, the justice asked his clerk to summarize evidence in the lower court trial record that demonstrated Garrison's malice and to prepare a possible footnote for inclusion in his concurring opinion. A few days later, the clerk delivered a sharply worded statement that insisted if Louisiana had tried Garrison under the *Times* rule, the Supreme Court "would be powerless" to overturn the conviction. Garrison's statements were false, and his continued public criticisms of the judges proved malice, the clerk wrote. Some of Garrison's comments were contradictory and demonstrated—at least to the clerk—a measure of guilt. Finally, as district attorney, Garrison had failed to use legal remedies at his disposal to investigate the truth of his accusations. Instead, he had attacked the judges in the press. "In sum, though the evidence of 'malice' in this case is not strong, I am afraid it is quite strong enough," the clerk concluded. Douglas never included the explosive footnote in his opinion, and the appearance of unanimity remained intact. Had he done so, it would have seriously undercut the majority opinion and left some wondering why the Supreme Court had used Garrison's case, with its malevolent underbelly, to protect the fundamental right of free speech.[21]

When Black joined Douglas' concurring opinion, he explained to his longtime First Amendment ally that he wanted to write a separate, similar opinion to emphasize "our objection to what is being done to the First Amendment." As he had expressed in a concurring opinion in *Times*, Black believed that neither the states nor Congress had the constitutional right to pass laws limiting free speech. He wanted the court to strike down all libel laws, and in the first draft of his concurring opinion in *Garrison*, Black summarized his absolutist views. "I believe that the First Amendment . . . permits every person in the country to say whatever he pleases about anyone on any subject without fear" of prosecution, the justice explained. In a successive draft, Black scaled back his unconditional stance, but the sentiment remained unchanged. The First Amendment, he insisted, protects a person when "he has been guilty of no other conduct other than expressing an opinion." Black concluded that libel laws hindered public discussion, an unfortunate result in a nation "dedicated as it is to liberty of the individual." To Black and Douglas, individual liberty included the right to speak without restriction from libel laws, either civil or criminal. It was a position both espoused consistently during their Supreme Court tenures and again stated in separate concurring opinions in *Garrison v. Louisiana*.[22]

On November 20, Brennan announced to the weekly conference that he was ready to release the court's unanimous opinion. Justices Black, Douglas, and Goldberg also indicated to the chief justice that their separate concurrences were ready for release. At 10 a.m. the following Monday, November 23, the robed justices entered the marbled courtroom from behind a scarlet red curtain. At 10:40 a.m., Warren announced the court had rendered a verdict in the case of *Garrison v. Louisiana*. He then turned to Justice Brennan, who began reading: "Appellant is the District Attorney of Orleans Parish, Louisiana . . ." No one in the audience knew that for eight months Brennan had worked toward this moment. No one knew how close Jim Garrison's appeal had come to failing, how the justices themselves had doubted his innocence, or how the second round of deliberations—and the disparate oral argument performances of Deutsch and Gremillion—ultimately had salvaged Garrison's appeal. As Brennan continued, however, one thing became evident: The *Garrison* case, like the *Times* decision that preceded it, was destined for landmark status. In overturning Garrison's conviction and ruling parts of the Louisiana defamation statute unconstitutional, the Supreme Court extended the *Times* actual malice standard to criminal and civil libel alike. It removed the wall between an official's public duties and his private life and enhanced the scope of acceptable criticism. Finally, and more importantly, the justices unambiguously embraced dissent as "the essence of self-government" in the United States. With that statement, Garrison's Bourbon Street imbroglio over money and influence was reborn as a First Amendment milestone.[23]

CONCLUSION

What It Meant:
The Legacy of *Garrison v. Louisiana*

When word reached Jim Garrison that the U.S. Supreme Court had overturned his defamation conviction, he responded characteristically. He issued a press release. With his typical rapier-like sarcasm, Garrison swatted Attorney General Jack Gremillion, who had prosecuted the case, Judge William Ponder, who had tried the lower court proceedings, and the justices of the Louisiana Supreme Court, who had affirmed his conviction. These men, Garrison chortled, "did not share my faith in the United States Constitution." The First Amendment guarantees "that in this country you can not prevent any citizen from speaking freely," the district attorney insisted, adding that these free speech protections were "not apparent to these gentlemen." He concluded his statement by musing that perhaps his prosecution had been "a good thing . . . Not only has it been reaffirmed that everyone has the right to criticize his public officials without being thrown into the dungeon, but the attorney general of Louisiana and the Supreme Court of Louisiana have learned something about the rights of American citizens." The press release, which the *Times-Picayune* published alongside the complete text of the Supreme Court's opinion, was typically Garrison—brash, provocative, and overstated. Garrison never spent time in "the dungeon" subsequent to his conviction. In fact, if any group now found itself shackled, it was Garrison's political enemies, who realized that the prosecutor's victory before the U.S. Supreme Court only strengthened his already solid political celebrity.[1]

Garrison's popularity with the New Orleans electorate had increased steadily during the twenty-month period that separated his defamation trial and the Supreme Court's decision. By November 1964, when the high court overturned Garrison's conviction, the district attorney had replaced two antagonistic Orleans Parish criminal district judges with his own candidates. He had helped John J. McKeithen carry New Orleans over former Mayor deLesseps S. Morrison in the 1964 Louisiana gubernatorial race and had considered running for attorney general against Jack Gremillion in the same election. Finally, in what he characterized as a stand for First Amendment rights, Garrison had stared down the White Citizen's Council and New Orleans Mayor Victor H. Schiro, who had lauded the arrest of a New Orleans bookstore owner for selling *Another Country*, a novel by black author James Baldwin. With each successive controversy, Garrison's electoral popularity grew, and his Supreme Court victory merely cemented what New Orleans political commentators now called the district attorney's "Midas touch in local politics."[2]

The U.S. Supreme Court's decision offered Garrison the political validation he had sought so earnestly—and maliciously—since becoming New Orleans district attorney two years before. Garrison characterized the defamation charges the judges had filed against him as yet another in a string of crusades he had fought on the public's behalf. He had confronted prostitutes, bar owners, and ethically challenged judges who represented New Orleans' political elite. Now, he would rise to defend the First Amendment right of free speech. Yet, in true Garrison fashion, the district attorney had manipulated reality. His self-portrayal as a defender of the public trust disguised Garrison's true crusade for political power. With *Garrison v. Louisiana*, the U.S. Supreme Court delivered a significant expansion of the right of free speech and allowed Garrison to add First Amendment crusader to his already formidable—albeit flawed—political résumé.[3]

The court issued its *Garrison* decision eight months after it ruled in *New York Times v. Sullivan*, and the role the later case played in augmenting the *Times* judgment remains its unquestioned legacy. Along with the extension of the *Times* actual malice rule to govern criminal libel cases, the significance of the *Garrison* case lies in three tenets that expanded a citizen's right to criticize public officials and limited the possibility of legal repercussions. First, the Supreme Court said that the public is entitled to evaluate even a public official's private life to determine his fitness for office. Second, in order to receive damages, a public official could not argue that his accuser did not have a reasonable belief in the truth of his statements; instead, he must prove actual malice as the court had defined in *Times*. Finally, the court differentiated between negligence and recklessness in proving intent to defame. The *Times* actual malice standard made reckless disregard for the truth punishable, but the court held in *Garrison* that negligence alone did not satisfy the *Times* test. The three maxims that *Garrison* set forth enhanced an uninhibited discourse on public affairs through mutual criticism and solidified the case's status as a First Amendment landmark.[4]

In determining the first of these three milestone provisions, the court weighed the right of a public official to protect his private reputation against the public's right to an unfettered discussion of public affairs. In justifying the court's decision that said a public official could no longer protect his private life through criminal libel suits, Justice William J. Brennan insisted that very little separated an official's private life from his public reputation. Criticism of one invariably will affect the other, Brennan concluded, and therefore the court could not limit a citizen's access to information about a public official's private life without affecting his ability to determine that official's fitness for office. With *Garrison*, the court expanded the "public official rule" it had established in *Times*. Brennan maintained that the standard intended to protect "the paramount public interest in a free flow of information to the people concerning public officials, their servants." He added that "anything which might touch on an official's fitness for public office is relevant," even if these characteristics affected his private reputation as well. With this first provision, the court effectively dismantled the barrier between officials' public and private lives. To do otherwise, the court ruled, would hinder a robust discussion of public affairs and would provide elected leaders an immunity from criticism that opposed the First Amendment's free speech clause.[5]

The second major provision *Garrison* established, which eradicated the reasonable belief argument long used in libel cases, was a vehicle by which the court reaffirmed the actual malice standard it set forth in *Times*. While rendering a guilty verdict in Garrison's lower court trial, the judge had included in his ruling a statement that the district attorney did not "reasonably believe" all eight criminal court judges were beholden to racketeers. The *Times* standard, however, was predicated on reckless disregard of the truth, not reasonable belief, Brennan wrote. The two standards simply were not analogous. The justice insisted that only calculated falsehoods, statements made with knowledge that they were false, lost constitutional protection. "Debate on public issues will not be uninhibited if the speaker must run the risk that it will be proved in court that he spoke out of hatred; even if he did speak out of hatred, utterances honestly believed contribute to the free exchange of ideas and the ascertainment of the truth," Brennan maintained. Furthermore, the *Garrison* ruling firmly defined the "reckless disregard of the truth" provision in the *Times* actual malice standard. In *Garrison,* Brennan analogized that phrase with another—"calculated falsehood." Both essentially meant the same thing—a deliberate lie—and neither enjoyed constitutional protection, he wrote. "For the use of the known lie as a tool is at once at odds with the premises of democratic government and with the orderly manner in which economic, social, or political change is to be effected," the justice concluded. With that, the Supreme Court used the second provision in its *Garrison* ruling to reaffirm and to clarify its earlier *Times* decision. It eradicated the "reasonable belief" argument and cemented the court's position that deliberate lies undermined the principles of the First Amendment.[6]

The final *Garrison* provision, like the second, dealt in semantics, and helped the Supreme Court clarify its earlier *Times* ruling. The *Times* actual malice standard made reckless disregard for the truth punishable. In *Garrison,* the court held that negligence alone did not satisfy the *Times* test. Legal scholars would later interpret this provision to apply not so much to libel suits emanating from speech, but rather those resulting from publication or broadcast. In the final tenet, the court said that the negligent failure of a speaker or publisher to check the accuracy of a statement prior to publication did not satisfy the *Times* rule's "reckless disregard" provision. "The test which we laid down in *New York Times* is not keyed to ordinary care," Brennan wrote, explaining, "defeasance of the privilege is conditioned, not on mere negligence, but on reckless disregard for the truth." In short, mere carelessness did not satisfy the "reckless disregard" requirements the court mandated in *Times.* This final maxim, combined with the eradication of the wall surrounding a public figure's private life, and the clarification of what constituted a calculated falsehood, played a pivotal role in removing barriers to an uninhibited and robust public discourse. Furthermore, the *Garrison* ruling provided guideposts for the court as it continued over the next decade to enlarge the limits of public debate and to erode legal recourse through libel actions.[7]

With its *Garrison* decision, the Supreme Court applied a uniform criterion to test both civil and criminal libel, yet questions remained unanswered. Although the court's decisions in *Times* and *Garrison* certainly overturned a major premise of its 1952 decision in *Beauharnais v. Illinois*—that libelous statements fell outside of the First Amendment's protection—the cases did not strike down the earlier ruling entirely. In *Beauharnais*, the court had upheld a group libel action; neither the *Times* nor *Garrison* cases overturned the areas of *Beauharnais* that made recovery of damages in group libel actions possible. Although weakened significantly by the court's later affirmations protecting criticism of public officials, the possibility of criminal lawsuits for group libel set forth in *Beauharnais* remains viable. *Garrison* left more significant questions unanswered, however, including who qualifies as a "public official." In both the *Times* and *Garrison* cases, the court dealt with libel against elected officeholders—a police commissioner and a group of judges, respectively. Yet in both cases, the court failed to indicate whether it included criticism of non-elected government officials or if the protections extended to criticism of "public figures," individuals outside of government service who nevertheless commanded intense public attention. In addition, the court did not decide if the actual malice standard also applied to candidates for public office. After the *Garrison* ruling, for example, a non-elected government employee could claim a critic had libeled him and the actual malice standard would be inapplicable. Furthermore, it would be incumbent upon the defendant to prove the official's position in the government was important enough to warrant protection under the actual malice defense. Therein lay another unanswered question; in *Garrison*, the court held that "anything which might touch on an official's fitness for office" was privileged criticism and therefore deserving of protection under the actual malice standard. Such criticism included criticism of an official's "dishonesty, malfeasance, or improper motivation," the court had stated. Some scholars argued after the *Garrison* ruling that the court's enumeration of those specific criticisms had two effects. The first was that a plaintiff could claim the criticism of his official conduct was not in reference to any of those three specific issues. Conversely, others argued those definite issues were too broad and gave defendants an unfair advantage. They simply had to show their criticisms fell within those guidelines in order to trigger the actual malice protections, thereby making it increasingly difficult for a public official to regain damages for unwarranted criticism.[8]

In the decade following its *Garrison* ruling, the court answered many of these questions, but only in relation to civil libel actions. In a ten-year span ending in 1974, the court continued to redefine and to extend the actual malice standard in the cases of *Rosenblatt v. Baer* (1966), *Curtis Publishing Co. v. Butts* (1967), *Rosenbloom v. Metromedia, Monitor Patriot Co. v. Roy* (both 1971), and *Gertz v. Welch* (1974). As progeny of the *Times* decision, each of these cases continued to extend the *Times* actual malice rule—and First Amendment protection—to areas of civil libel, while criminal defamation remained viable. Since *Garrison*, the court has considered only one criminal defamation case, but its ruling in *Ashton v. Kentucky* (1966) merely reinforced the *Garrison* precedent by again cautioning state legislatures to construct libel laws narrowly. Because no further criminal libel actions have come before the court, however, and because neither the *Garrison* nor *Ashton* rulings struck down criminal defamation laws entirely, prosecutions for criminal defamation persist.[9]

In its 1974 ruling in *Gertz v. Welch*, the Supreme Court extended the actual malice provision to include civil libel actions brought by private individuals. The court's rulings prior to *Gertz* in *Rosenblatt v. Baer, Curtis Publishing Co. v. Butts, Rosenbloom v. Metromedia*, and *Monitor Patriot v. Roy* had applied only to civil libel cases involving public persons. This succession of cases that extended the actual malice rule in civil libel actions to encompass both public and private individuals has yet to occur in the arena of criminal libel. In 2003, the First Circuit Court of Appeals noted this dissonance when it held that "criminal libel statutes share the constitutional limitations of civil libel law." Yet because of the lack of Supreme Court precedent, and the continued existence of state defamation laws, prosecutions for criminal libel against both public and private individuals continue unabated. Admittedly, since the *Garrison* ruling in 1964, instances of criminal defamation prosecutions have dropped significantly. Between 1916 and 1965, there were 148 criminal libel prosecutions in the United States. Since the *Garrison* ruling, only seventy-seven such charges have been filed. According to a 2003 report by the Media Law

Resource Center, about fifty of those seventy-seven cases involved contentious partisan issues and were blatant in their use of criminal defamation as a retaliatory political weapon. Without a clear mandate from the federal courts that offers guidance to govern criminal libel actions against private and public figures alike, such defamation prosecutions remain viable and constitutionally legitimate.[10]

As of 2009, seventeen states and two U.S. territories retained criminal defamation laws written prior to the *Garrison* decision. State courts have upheld many of these statutes as functional in criminal suits brought by private individuals, and because the U.S. Supreme Court has taken no further action in the field of criminal defamation laws, these statutes remain constitutional. Louisiana, the birthplace of the *Garrison* decision, serves as an example of this dynamic. As of 2009, the Louisiana defamation statute under which the state prosecuted Jim Garrison remains in effect, despite the U.S. Supreme Court decision that held portions of it unconstitutional. In *Garrison v. Louisiana*, the court labeled the Louisiana law as inconsistent with the actual malice test it had established in the *Times* ruling. The court's decision applied only to criticism of public officials' conduct, however, and it left unclear whether Louisiana could use the statute to punish private defamation. In 1970, the U.S. District Court for the Western District of Louisiana ruled that the defamation statute was not unconstitutional *per se* and suggested the state courts and the Legislature revisit the provisions that made the law inconsistent with the *Times* actual malice standard. The federal court further explained that the *Garrison* decision had struck down the statute as it applied to public officials, but had not prohibited its use in private libel cases. Without comment, the U.S. Supreme Court later affirmed the lower court's decision.[11] In 1973, the Louisiana Supreme Court similarly held that the defamation statute remained viable in private defamation matters.[12]

As the Supreme Court issued decisions between 1964 and 1974 building on the expansion of First Amendment rights it had begun in the *Times* and *Garrison* rulings, Jim Garrison's attention was elsewhere. In an article in *New Orleans* magazine published during this period, writer David Chandler described Garrison as sullen and withdrawn. Chandler asked Garrison why there had been no recent raids on Bourbon Street clip joints, no crackdowns on prostitution, or none of the other colorful, flamboyant events that had characterized the prosecutor's early days in office. "Why bother?" Garrison complained. "I cleaned up Bourbon Street and I didn't get any credit. I never get any credit. Another reason we don't have fights anymore is because we've beaten the people trying to stop justice in New Orleans. I am in no fight because I have no opponents." As in previous statements, however, Garrison engaged in a bit of deception during his interview with Chandler. By November 1966, when the article was published, Garrison had taken on an opponent and a crusade that made his row with the judges seem tame. Garrison's investigation of the assassination of President John F. Kennedy redefined his career, elevated him again into the national media spotlight, and undermined the significance of the U.S. Supreme Court case that bore his name. Throughout the 1960s and early 1970s, as the Supreme Court continued to use the *Garrison* precedent to enhance public discourse, the New Orleans district attorney attempted to implicate the federal government's intelligence agencies in a plot to assassinate President Kennedy. Garrison theorized that several New Orleans residents, including Clay L. Shaw, once director of the city's International Trade Mart, conspired to kill the president. In 1969, Garrison brought Shaw to trial. After thirty-four days of testimony, a jury returned a not guilty verdict in less than an hour. Undeterred, Garrison accused Shaw of perjury and continued his attempts to prove the business executive's guilt until a U.S. District Court enjoined him from further prosecutions in 1971. In 1973, Garrison lost his bid for a fourth term as district attorney. Garrison practiced law in New Orleans until 1978, when voters elected him to the Louisiana Fourth Circuit Court of Appeal, where he served as a judge until he reached the state mandatory retirement age of seventy in 1991.[13]

For the remainder of his life and public career, Garrison continued to espouse conspiracy theories, most notably in three books: *A Heritage of Stone* (1970), *The Star Spangled Contract* (1974), a fictionalized account of a presidential murder, and *On the Trail of the Assassins*, released in 1988 to coincide with the twenty-fifth anniversary of Kennedy's death. The books, along with countless appearances on television documentaries, fueled the growth of the Garrison legend among those who saw him as a founding father in the ever-expanding network of conspiracy theorists. Others came to believe Garrison's futile Shaw prosecution only increased the federal government's determination to hide the truth about Kennedy's death. For that, they vilified the former prosecutor; the firestorm reached a new crescendo in the early 1990s when director Oliver Stone bought the rights to Garrison's memoir, *On the Trail of the Assassins,* and announced plans for a movie with Garrison as its central character.[14] Critics charged that the film, *JFK,* lionized Garrison while it criminalized Shaw. Others insisted the mixture of historical fact with supposition served only to imbue the nation's youth with a fictionalized portrayal of a tragic event. Ironically, Garrison, who had thrived throughout his career on controversy, remained largely secluded during the final tempest of his life. Ill and dying, the former district attorney appeared rarely in public, although he had a cameo in the film, ironically, as Chief Justice Earl Warren, who headed the investigatory commission whose conclusions Garrison once criticized so vehemently. When Garrison died on October 21, 1992, few obituaries mentioned the 1964 U.S. Supreme Court case that, along with *New York Times v. Sullivan,* expanded the scope of public criticism in the United States. Only Garrison's hometown newspaper, the *Times-Picayune,* dedicated more than a single line to the case, but even its report focused on the colorful details of the case's origins and not the legal realities that resulted. In an obituary in the *New Yorker,* Edward Jay Epstein, whose 1966 book *Inquest* was among the first wave of critical appraisals of the Warren Commission, packed into two sentences both the case's beginnings and its significance to free speech. Epstein devoted the remainder of his five thousand-word remembrance to his own observations of Garrison's Kennedy probe. No mentions of the case appeared in the *New York Times, Washington Post,* or Associated Press obituaries. All focused instead on the Shaw prosecution. In death, the press remembered Jim Garrison not for the case he won, but for the one he lost.[15]

By ignoring *Garrison v. Louisiana* in their obituaries of the former district attorney, the journalists failed to grasp the significance the decision had on Garrison's career and on the elemental right of free speech in the United States. With its *Garrison* ruling, the U.S. Supreme Court handed the New Orleans prosecutor a personal victory, one that he used to cement his formidable hold on the city's political landscape. Of greater significance is the case's continued importance to an uninhibited discourse on public affairs. By limiting the ability of public officials to retaliate through prosecutions for criminal defamation, *Garrison v. Louisiana* expanded an individual's First Amendment right to criticize government. With its characterization of public criticism as "the essence of self-government," the court transformed a provincial political squabble into an affirmation of a fundamentally American right. Within the marbled halls of the U.S. Supreme Court, *Garrison v. Louisiana* ceased to be a fight about finances. Instead, it became about freedom.[16]

Notes

Introduction

1. Rosemary James and Jack Wardlaw, *Plot or Politics? The Garrison Case and Its Cast* (New Orleans: Pelican Publishing House, 1967), 19.

2. *Garrison v. Louisiana*, 379 U.S. 64 (1964), 66-67.

3. *New York Times v. Sullivan*, 376 U.S. 250 (1964), 279-80; and *Garrison v. Louisiana*, 74-75.

4. See, for example, "Battle over New Orleans Vice Pits Stubborn DA against Stubborn Judge," *Washington Post*, February 10, 1963; "District Attorney Convicted of Libel Takes Case against Jurists to Public," *Washington Post*, February 11, 1963; "New Orleans Morality Undermined by Link between Crime and Politics," *Washington Post*, February 12, 1963; "8 Judges in Feud with Prosecutor," *New York Times*, November 11, 1962; "Case of the Crusading DA," *Newsweek*, February 18, 1963, 26; James Phelan, "The Vice Man Cometh," *Saturday Evening Post*, June 8, 1963, 67-71; and Jack Wardlaw, "A Crusading DA and His Eight Foes: The Judges," *National Observer*, January 29, 1963, 3. See also Gene Roberts, "The Case of Jim Garrison and Lee Oswald," *New York Times Magazine*, May 21, 1967, 40; James and Wardlaw, *Plot or Politics?*, 27; and Milton E. Brener, *The Garrison Case: A Study in the Abuse of Power* (New York: Clarkson E. Potter, 1969), 6.

5. Patricia Lambert, *False Witness: The Real Story of Jim Garrison's Investigation and Oliver Stone's Film JFK* (New York: M. Evans, 1998), xiv.

6. James and Wardlaw, *Plot or Politics?*, 16-22; James Kirkwood, *American Grotesque: An Account of the Clay Shaw-Jim Garrison Affair in the City of New Orleans* (New York: Simon and Schuster, 1970), 471-72, 576-77.

7. See, for example, W. Wat Hopkins, *Actual Malice: Twenty-Five Years after Times v. Sullivan* (New York: Praeger, 1989); and Anthony Lewis, *Make No Law: The Sullivan Case and the First Amendment* (New York: Vintage Books, 1992).

8. Records of the United States Supreme Court, RG 267, National Archives and Records Administration, Washington, D.C.; *New Orleans Times-Picayune*, August 1962-November 1964; Records of the New Orleans Metropolitan Crime Commission, RG 541, President John F. Kennedy

Assassinations Records Collection, National Archives and Records Administration, College Park, MD; United States Supreme Court, *Records and Briefs* (California, MD: Congressional Information Service, 1964), microfiche; *State of Louisiana v. Jim Garrison*, files of the Orleans Parish Criminal District Court, New Orleans, microfilm; *State of Louisiana v. Jim Garrison*, Office of the Clerk of Court, Supreme Court of Louisiana, New Orleans, microfilm; James and Wardlaw, *Plot or Politics?*; and Brener, *The Garrison Case*.

9. This study utilizes the available records of seven of nine Warren Court justices. The Library of Congress houses the files of Chief Justice Earl Warren and associate justices Hugo L. Black, William J. Brennan Jr., William O. Douglas, Arthur J. Goldberg Jr., and Byron R. White. White's records are restricted and inaccessible, as are those of Justice Potter Stewart at Yale University. The University of Texas at Austin is the repository for Justice Tom C. Clark's files, while Princeton retains the papers of Justice John Marshall Harlan II. See also Oral Arguments of *Garrison v. Louisiana*, 22 April 1964, Case #400, Record #267.512, Sound Recordings from the National Archives and Records Administration; and Oral Arguments of *Garrison v. Louisiana*, 22 April 1964, Case #4, Record #267.496, Sound Recordings from the National Archives and Records Administration.

10. Clifton O. Lawhorne, *Defamation and Public Officials: The Evolving Law of Libel* (Carbondale: Southern Illinois University Press, 1971); Clifton O. Lawhorne, *The Supreme Court and Libel* (Carbondale: Southern Illinois University Press, 1981); Thomas L. Tedford, *Freedom of Speech in the United States*, 3d ed. (State College, Pa.: Strata Publishing, 1997); Ronald L. Naquin, "Constitutional Law—Freedom of Speech—Defamation," *Tulane Law Review* 39 (February 1965): 355-62; Thomas I. Emerson, *The System of Freedom of Expression* (New York: Random House, 1970); Thomas I. Emerson, *Toward a General Theory of the First Amendment* (New York: Random House, 1966); James DiEugenio, *Destiny Betrayed: JFK, Cuba, and the Garrison Case* (New York: Sheridan Square Press, 1992), 127-28; Lambert, *False Witness*, 17-20; and Joan Mellen, *A Farewell to Justice: Jim Garrison, JFK's Assassination, and the Case that Should Have Changed History* (Dulles, Va.: Potomac Books, 2005), 10, 17-20. Mellen's Garrison biography, *Jim Garrison: His Life and Times – The Early Years* (Southlake, Texas: JFK Lancer, 2008), gives more background into the case's origins than did her first work, but it offers only a scant examination of the implications of *Garrison v. Louisiana*.

11. Papers of Jim Garrison, RG 541, President John F. Kennedy Assassination Records Collection, National Archives and Records Administration, College Park, Md.; Jim Garrison, *A Heritage of Stone* (New York: G.P. Putnam's Sons, 1970); Jim Garrison, *The Star Spangled Contract* (New York: McGraw-Hill, 1976); and Jim Garrison, *On the Trail of the Assassins: My Investigation and Prosecution of the Murder of President Kennedy* (New York: Sheridan Square Press, 1988).

12. Garrison, *On the Trail of the Assassins*, xii.

Chapter I

1. James Phelan, "Vice Man Cometh," *Saturday Evening Post*, June 8, 1963, 70.

2. *Garrison v. Louisiana*, 379 U.S. 64 (1964).

3. Jim Garrison, "The Lawyer and the Bill of Rights," *American Criminal Law Quarterly* 3 (Fall 1964): 152, in folder "Jim Garrison," box 8, Investigative Files Received from New Orleans District Attorney Harry Connick, Papers of Jim Garrison, RG 541, President John F. Kennedy Assassination Records Collection, National Archives and Records Administration, College Park, MD [hereinafter cited as Garrison Papers, NARA].

4. "Witness in Night Club Padlocking Move Heard," *New Orleans Times-Picayune*, December 12, 1962; "DA to Ask Lock for Five Clubs," *Times-Picayune*, December 2, 1962; and "22 Women Face Morals Cases," *Times-Picayune*, December 4, 1962.

5. "Quarter Vice Drive Opened," *Times-Picayune*, August 7, 1962; and "Battle over New Orleans Vice Pits Stubborn DA against Stubborn Judge," *Washington Post*, February 10, 1963.

6. "Garrison Sees Strip Clubs' End," *Times-Picayune*, September 20, 1962; "Quarter Group Commends Garrison," *Times-Picayune*, August 31, 1962; "Vieux Carre Crackdown Needed," *Times-Picayune*, August 7. 1962; Executive Committee, Metropolitan Crime Commission of New Orleans Inc., to Jim Garrison, District Attorney, Parish of Orleans, August 23, 1962, folder "Criminal District Court," box 6, Records of the New Orleans Metropolitan Crime Commission, RG 541, President John F. Kennedy Assassination Records Collection, National Archives and Records Administration, College Park, MD [hereinafter cited as MCC Records, NARA]; and Phelan, "Vice Man Cometh," 70.

7. Phelan, "Vice Man Cometh," 68, 70; "Stripper Says N.O. Is Too Hot," *Times-Picayune*, August 27, 1962; "Halt Weighed by Night Clubs," *Times-Picayune*, September 6, 1962; and "Over 12 Bourbon St. Clubs Shut in Apparent Protest," *Times-Picayune*, September 24, 1962.

8. Christine Wiltz, *The Last Madam: A Life in the New Orleans Underworld* (New York: Da Capo Press, 2000), 142-43, 145; Gene Roberts, "The Case of Jim Garrison and Lee Oswald," *New York Times Magazine*, May 21, 1967, 32-33; Confidential Informant No. 1 to Aaron Kohn, "Investigative Report," March 8, 1958, and Aaron Kohn, "Investigative Report," January 15, 1963, both in folder "Jim Garrison, Orleans Parish District Attorney, Vol. No. 3," box 8, MCC Records, NARA; and "New Orleans Vice Pits Stubborn DA against Stubborn Judge," *Washington Post*, February 10, 1963.

9. *Acts of the Louisiana Legislature*, 301:16 (1946); "Mayor to Help DA in Cleanup," *Times-Picayune*, August 28, 1962; "D.A., Giarusso, Mayor to Talk," *Times-Picayune*, August 29, 1962; "Will Not Quarrel, Giarusso States," *Times-Picayune*, August 30, 1962; "First Daytime Raid is Made," *Times-Picayune*, August 31, 1962; and Milton E. Brener, *The Garrison Case: A Study in the Abuse of Power* (New York: Clarkson E. Potter, 1969), 22.

10. "Courts Function Despite Strife Sparked by Row," *New Orleans States-Item*, December 7, 1962, folder 1, box 5753, United States Supreme Court Appellate Case Files, RG 267, Records of the U.S. Supreme Court, National Archives and Records Administration, Washington, D.C. [hereinafter cited as U.S. Supreme Court Case Files, NARA]; and *Louisiana Revised Statutes*, 15:571.11 (1950).

11. "Judges Refuse to Okay Funds," *Times-Picayune*, August 21, 1962; Jim Garrison, *On the Trail of the Assassins: My Investigation and Prosecution of the Murder of President Kennedy* (New York: Sheridan Square Press, 1988), 12; "Jurists Question Expenditures in Garrison Office," *New Orleans States-Item*, December 5, 1962, folder 1, box 5753, U.S. Supreme Court Case Files, NARA; "DA Reports Budget Lowered," *Times-Picayune*, August 23, 1962; "D.A. Borrows to Aid Office," *Times-Picayune*, August 29, 1962; and Brener, *The Garrison Case*, 22.

12. *Times-Picayune*, September 1 - September 30, 1962; "Judges and DA Agree on Fund," *Times-Picayune*, October 5, 1962; "D.A. and Eight Judges Agree," *Times-Picayune*, October 6, 1962; Brener, *The Garrison Case*, 16; "Jurists Question Expenditures in Garrison Office," *New Orleans States-Item*, December 5, 1962, and Thomas M. Brahney, Jr. to Jim Garrison, October 26,

1962, both in folder 1, box 5753, U.S. Supreme Court Case Files, NARA.

13. "Prison Inmates above Capacity," *Times-Picayune*, October 26, 1962; "D.A. is Critical of N.O. Judges," *Times-Picayune*, November 1, 1962; and "Judge Views DA Accusation as 'Wild Charges,'" *Times-Picayune*, November 2, 1962.

14. Brener, *The Garrison Case*, 16-17; and Eberhard P. Deutsch, "From Zenger to Garrison: A Tale of Two Centuries," *New York State Bar Journal* 38 (October 1966): 412.

15. "Battle over New Orleans Vice Pits Stubborn DA against Stubborn Judge," *Washington Post*, February 10, 1963.

16. Brener, *The Garrison Case*, 16-17; and "Judge Views DA Accusations as 'Wild Charges,'" *Times-Picayune*, November 2, 1962.

17. "Judges Views DA Accusation as 'Wild Charges,'" *Times-Picayune*, November 2, 1962; "Testimony of Bert Hyde," January 21, 1963, 203-204, "Testimony of Arthur Roane," January 21, 1963, 222-23, and "Text of Garrison Stand on Judges," *New Orleans States-Item*, November 2, 1962, 27-30, all in U.S. Supreme Court, *Records and Briefs* (California, MD: Congressional Information Service, 1964), microfiche [hereinafter cited as *Records and Briefs*].

18. "Text of Garrison Stand on Judges," *New Orleans States-Item*, November 2, 1962, *Records and Briefs*, 27-30.

19. Ibid., 27-29.

20. "Judges Answer Garrison," *Times-Picayune*, November 3, 1962; and "Testimony of Bill Reed," January 21, 1963, *Records and Briefs*, 278-79.

21. "Garrison Answers Judges' Statement," *Times-Picayune*, November 3, 1962; "One Judge Idle Six Months–DA," *Times-Picayune*, November 4, 1962; "Cocke Explains Reasons for No Court on Fridays," *Times-Picayune*, November 5, 1962; and "Judges Gather, No Statement," *Times-Picayune*, November 6, 1962.

22. "Judges Angry with Garrison," *Times-Picayune*, November 8, 1962; "Garrison Top Aid Dismisses Charge," *Times-Picayune*, November 9, 1962; and "Ponder to Hear Garrison Case," *Times-Picayune*, November 14, 1962.

23. *Louisiana Revised Statutes*, 14:47 (1950).

24. Ibid.; and "Garrison Top Aid Dismisses Charge," *Times-Picayune*, November 9, 1962.

25. Brener, *The Garrison Case*, 19; and "Transcription of shorthand notes taken at the meeting held at St. Anthony's Auditorium on Wednesday, December 5, 1962, by Theresa E. Shean," folder 1, box 5753, U.S. Supreme Court Case Files, NARA.

26. Brener, *The Garrison Case*, 20-21; "Cocke Broke Secrecy, Grand Jury Contends," *Times-Picayune*, January 11, 1963; "Judge Indicted by Grand Jury," *Times-Picayune*, February 13, 1963; "Cocke Assails Letter from DA," *Times-Picayune*, August 16, 1962; and "Cocke Control of DA's Claimed," *Times-Picayune*, February 19, 1963.

27. Ironically, an Iberia Parish judge found Warren Moity guilty of defaming the parish's district attorney the same week Garrison was on trial. Moity had alleged the Iberia district attorney had imprisoned a black suspect although the prosecutor had known the testimony he had used to convict the man was false. In a *per curium* opinion, the U.S. Supreme Court overturned Moity's conviction on December 7, 1964 based on its earlier ruling in *Garrison v. Louisiana*. *Moity v. Louisiana*, 379 U.S. 201 (1964); and "Two in New Iberia Fined for Defamation of DA," *Times-Picayune*, February 7, 1963.

28. Brener, *The Garrison Case*, 21, 24, 33; Rosemary James and Jack Wardlaw, *Plot or Politics? The Garrison Case and Its Cast* (New Orleans: Pelican Publishing House, 1967), 99-102, 104-105; and J. Cleveland Frugé, *Biographies of Louisiana Judges* (n.p: Louisiana District Judges Association, 1961), 1-2.

Chapter II

1. Milton E. Brener, *The Garrison Case: A Study in the Abuse of Power* (New York: Clarkson E. Potter, 1969), 20.

2. "Judge Admits Attending Alleged Gambler's Party," *New Orleans Times-Picayune*, January 23, 1963; "Cocke Calls DA Prober 'Thief, Grafter, Ruffian,'" *Times-Picayune*, January 24, 1963; "Case of the Crusading DA," *Newsweek*, February 18, 1963, 26; and James Kirkwood, *American Grotesque: An Account of the Clay Shaw-Jim Garrison Affair in the City of New Orleans* (New York: Simon & Schuster, 1970), 178.

3. Brener, *The Garrison Case*, 20.

4. "Garrison Asks Open Hearing," *Times-Picayune*, November 15, 1962; "Public Hearing Motion is Filed by DA Garrison," *Times-Picayune*, November 17, 1962; "Garrison Trial to Begin Jan. 21," *Times-Picayune*, December 18, 1962; Louisiana Constitution (1921), art. 7, sec. 42; "Motion for Trial by Jury," December 5, 1962, in U.S. Supreme Court, *Records and Briefs* (California, MD: Congressional Information Service, 1964), microfiche [hereinafter cited as *Records and Briefs*], 38; "Motion of Jim Garrison to recuse William H. Ponder, trial judge," "Demurrer and Motion to Quash," and "Application for a Bill of Particulars," December 4, 1962, *Records and Briefs*, 33-37; and "DA Asks Charges Quashed," *Times-Picayune*, December 5, 1962.

5. "Garrison Tells of Grievances," *Times-Picayune*, November 15, 1962; "DA Won't Issue Public Apology," *Times-Picayune*, January 12, 1963; "Judges Tighten Spending by DA," *Times-Picayune*, January 10, 1963; "Transcription of shorthand notes taken at the meeting held at St. Anthony's Auditorium on Wednesday, December 5, 1962, by Theresa E. Shean," folder 1, box 5753, United States Supreme Court Appellate Case Files, RG 267, National Archives and Records Administration, Washington, D.C. [hereinafter cited as U.S. Supreme Court Case Files, NARA]; and *Louisiana Revised Statutes* 14:47-14:50 (1950).

6. "O'Hara Denies Any Rackets Influence," *Times-Picayune*, January 22, 1963; "Judge Admits Attending Alleged Gambler's Party," *Times-Picayune*, January 23, 1963; "Cocke Calls DA Prober 'Thief, Grafter, Ruffian,'" *Times-Picayune*, January 24, 1963; and "Argument Delayed in Garrison Trial," *Times-Picayune*, January 25, 1963.

7. "O'Hara Denies Any Rackets Influence," *Times-Picayune*, January 22, 1963; Rosemary James and Jack Wardlaw, *Plot or Politics? The Garrison Case and Its Cast* (New Orleans: Pelican Publishing House, 1967), 102; "Investigative Report," from Confidential Informant No. 1 to Aaron Kohn, March 8, 1958, folder "Jim Garrison, Orleans Parish District Attorney, Vol. No. 3," box 8, Records of the New Orleans Metropolitan Crime Commission, RG 541, National Archives and Records Administration, College Park, MD [hereinafter cited as MCC Records, NARA]; *Louisiana Revised Statutes*, 14:47-14:50 (1950); and "Testimony of Judge Malcolm V. O'Hara," January 21, 1963, *Records and Briefs*, 286.

8. "Testimony of Judge William J. O'Hara," January 22, 1963, *Records*

and Briefs, 322; and "Judge Admits Attending Alleged Gambler's Party," *Times-Picayune,* January 23, 1963.

9. "Judge Admits Attending Alleged Gambler's Party," *Times-Picayune,* January 23, 1963; "Testimony of Judge William J. O'Hara," January 22, 1963, *Records and Briefs,* 322, 327, 329-331; "Motion," December 7, 1959, and "Re: Purchase of New Automobiles for Use by District Attorney," November 18, 1960, both in folder 1, box 5753, U.S. Supreme Court Case Files, NARA.

10. "Testimony of Judge Shirley G. Wimberly," January 22, 1963, *Records and Briefs,* 348-50, 358-61; and J. Cleveland Frugé, *Biographies of Louisiana Judges* (n.p: Louisiana District Judges Association, 1961), 113.

11. "Testimony of Judge Shirley G. Wimberly," January 22, 1963, *Records and Briefs,* 362-63.

12. Ibid., 367-68, 373, 375; and "Judge Admits Attending Alleged Gambler's Party," *Times-Picayune,* January 23, 1963.

13. "Testimony of Judge Oliver P. Schulingkamp," January 22, 1963, *Records and Briefs,* 387, 392, 394; and "Judge Admits Attending Alleged Gambler's Party," *Times-Picayune,* January 23, 1963.

14. "Testimony of Judge Edward A. Haggerty, Jr.," January 22-23, 1963, *Records and Briefs,* 413-14, 445-46; and "Cocke Calls DA Prober 'Thief, Grafter, Ruffian,'" *Times-Picayune,* January 24, 1963.

15. "Testimony of Judge Edward A. Haggerty, Jr.," January 22-23, 1963, *Records and Briefs,* 447, 453-56.

16. "Testimony of Judge Thomas M. Brahney, Jr.," 517-22, and "Testimony of Judge Bernard J. Bagert, Jr.," January 23, 1963, both in *Records and Briefs,* 479.

17. "Cocke Calls DA Prober 'Thief, Grafter, Ruffian,'" *Times-Picayune,* January 24, 1963; "Testimony of Judge George W. Platt," January 23, 1963, *Records and Briefs,* 496-97; and Mrs. G.W. Platt to Eugene J. Philastre, March 16, 1946, folder 1, box 5753, U.S. Supreme Court Case Files, NARA.

18. "Testimony of Judge J. Bernard Cocke," January 23-24, 1963, *Records and Briefs,* 527, 528-29, 531-32, 545-47; and "Cocke Assails Letter from DA," *Times-Picayune,* August 16, 1962.

19. "Testimony of Judge J. Bernard Cocke," January 23-24, 1963, *Records and Briefs*, 548.

20. "Testimony of Joseph I. Giarusso," January 24, 1963, *Records and Briefs*, 563-65; Brener, *The Garrison Case*, 20; and "O'Hara Denies Any Rackets Influence," *Times-Picayune*, January 22, 1963.

21. "Argument Delayed in Garrison Trial," *Times-Picayune*, January 25, 1963; "Garrison Decision is Due Wednesday," *Times-Picayune*, February 5, 1963; and "Opening Argument by Plaintiff," February 4, 1963, *Records and Briefs*, 587-89.

22. "Argument by the Defendant," February 4, 1963, *Records and Briefs*, 593, 601-602.

23. "Opinion," February 6, 1963, *Records and Briefs*, 625-29; and *Garrison v. Louisiana*, 379 U.S. 64 (1964), 78-79.

24. Phelan, "Vice Man Cometh," 70; "Continuing Crime Fight— Garrison," *Times-Picayune*, February 7, 1963; "Garrison Fined $1000; Appeal Notice Filed," *Times-Picayune*, March 1, 1963; and "Motion for Appeal to the Supreme Court of Louisiana and Order Thereon," February 28, 1963, *Records and Briefs*, 60-61; James and Wardlaw, *Plot or Politics?*, 22; and David Chandler, "The Devil's DA," *New Orleans* (November 1966), 32.

25. "Original Brief on Behalf of Jim Garrison, Appellant," May 1963, files of the Supreme Court of Louisiana, f46672-46688, reel #665, Clerk of Court, Supreme Court of Louisiana, New Orleans, 30.

Chapter III

1. Garrison's first assistant district attorney initially dismissed the charges against his boss, but the judges asked state Attorney General Jack Gremillion to reinstate them. See chapter one.

2. "Motion of Jim Garrison to Recuse the Honorable William H. Ponder, Trial Judge," December 4, 1962, in U.S. Supreme Court, *Records and Briefs* (California, MD: Congressional Information Service, 1964), microfiche [hereinafter cited as *Records and Briefs*], 33; and "Original Brief on Behalf of Jim Garrison, Appellant," May 1963, files of the Supreme Court of Louisiana, f46672-46688, reel #665, Clerk of Court, Supreme Court of Louisiana, New Orleans [hereinafter cited as Garrison brief, Louisiana Supreme Court], 17, 28-29.

3. *Gideon v. Wainwright*, 372 U.S. 335 (1963); and Garrison brief, Louisiana Supreme Court, 72-75.

4. Garrison brief, Louisiana Supreme Court, 76-83; and Stephen B. Presser and Jamil S. Zainaldin, *Law and Jurisprudence in American History: Cases and Comment*, 4th ed. American Casebook Series, ed. Jesse H. Choper, et al. (St. Paul, MN: West Group, 2000), 31-48.

5. Garrison brief, Louisiana Supreme Court, 34-40; Louisiana Constitution (1921), art. 1, sec. 3; Zechariah Chafee, Jr., *Free Speech in the United States* (Cambridge, MA: Harvard University Press, 1946), 21; and John P. Frank, "Hugo L. Black: Free Speech and the Declaration of Independence," in Ronald Rotunda, ed., *Six Justices on Civil Rights* (New York: Oceana Publications, 1983), 11-12.

6. *Schenck v. U.S.*, 249 U.S. 47 (1919); and Garrison brief, Louisiana Supreme Court, 49-54.

7. *Wood v. Georgia*, 370 U.S. 375 (1962), quoted in Garrison brief, Louisiana Supreme Court, 69-70; and *Louisiana Revised Statutes* 14:49 (1950).

8. *Thornhill v. Alabama*, 310 U.S. 88 (1940), quoted in Garrison brief, Louisiana Supreme Court, 40-41; and Ibid., 34-40, 42-43.

9. "Original Brief on Behalf of the State of Louisiana, Appellee," May 1963, files of the Supreme Court of Louisiana, f46672-46688, reel #665, Clerk of Court, Supreme Court of Louisiana, New Orleans [hereinafter cited as Attorney General's brief, Louisiana Supreme Court], 3-7.

10. *State of Louisiana v. Livaudais*, 161 La. 886 (1926), quoted in Attorney General's brief, Louisiana Supreme Court, 20-21; and Ibid., 8-9.

11. Attorney General's brief, Louisiana Supreme Court, 13-20.

12. Garrison brief, Louisiana Supreme Court, 31-70; and Attorney General's brief, Louisiana Supreme Court, 35-38, 42-43.

13. The description here of oral arguments before the Louisiana Supreme Court relies on contemporary newspaper coverage, not official court transcripts. According to a librarian at the Louisiana Supreme Court, transcriptions of oral arguments during the period the court heard the *Garrison* case were ordered only at the request of one of the parties involved

in the litigation. Furthermore, according to a respected guidebook, the U.S. Supreme Court did not require the arguments be included in the lower court record it reviewed once it had granted an appeal. Therefore, it is unlikely that either the state or the defense asked for a transcription. "Court Hears Arguments on Appeal by Garrison," *New Orleans Times-Picayune*, 4 May 1963; Robert L. Stern and Eugene Gressman, *Supreme Court Practice*, 3rd ed. (Washington, D.C.: BNA Incorporated, 1962), 100; and "Official Docket, Supreme Court of Louisiana, posted Monday, March 11, 1963," folder 2 "Court Business 1963," box 9, John B. Fournet Papers, Mss. 2558, Louisiana and Lower Mississippi Valley Collections, Louisiana State University, Baton Rouge [hereinafter cited as Fournet Papers, LSU].

14. Warren M. Billings, "The Supreme Court of Louisiana and the Administration of Justice, 1813-1995," *Louisiana History* 37 (Fall 1996): 400; J. Cleveland Frugé, *Biographies of Louisiana Judges* (n.p: Louisiana District Judges Association, 1965), 9-10, 15-16; *State of Louisiana v. Jim Garrison*, 244 La. 787 (1963) [hereinafter cited as *State v. Garrison*], 839-43; *Betts v. Brady*, 316 U.S. 455 (1942), quoted in *State v. Garrison*, 840-41.

15. *Beauharnais v. Illinois*, 343 U.S. 250 (1952), quoted in *State v. Garrison*, 827-28; and Ibid., 824-33, 871-77.

16. "Court Upholds D.A. Conviction," *Times-Picayune*, June 5, 1963; and "Application for Rehearing," June 17, 1963, folder 3, box 5753, United States Supreme Court Appellate Case Files, RG 267, National Archives and Records Administration, Washington, D.C. [hereinafter cited as U.S. Supreme Court Case Files, NARA].

17. "Application for Rehearing," June 17, 1963, "Petition for Supersedeas, Stay of Execution and Recall of Mandate," June 28, 1963, "Order for Supersedeas, Stay of Execution and Recall of Mandate," June 28, 1963, and "Notice of Appeal to the Supreme Court of the United States," July 11, 1963, all in folder 3, box 5753, U.S. Supreme Court Case Files, NARA.

18. In *A Farewell to Justice*, author Joan Mellen insists Deutsch, eager for the spotlight, muscled his way into the case. Mellen makes these assertions without citation, and it is unlikely an attorney of Deutsch's international stature would insist on arguing a criminal libel case before the U.S. Supreme Court when he had built his practice and reputation on civil cases. It is more likely that Deutsch simply was helping his friend Garrison, who had worked in Deutsch's New Orleans law firm in the early 1950s and for whom Garrison later named one of his sons. Joan Mellen, *A Farewell to Justice: Jim Garrison,*

JFK's Assassination, and the Case that Should Have Changed History (Dulles, VA: Potomac Books, 2005), 5-6, 19. See also Joan Mellen, *Jim Garrison: His Life and Times—The Early Years* (Southlake, Texas: JFK Lancer, 2008), 137-40; "Col. Deutsch Dead at Age 82," *Times-Picayune,* January 17, 1980; "E.P. Deutsch, a Louisiana Lawyer," *New York Times,* January 18, 1980; *Grosjean v. American Press Co.,* 297 U.S. 233 (1936); Richard C. Cortner, *The Kingfish and the Constitution: Huey Long, the First Amendment, and the Emergence of Modern Press Freedom in America.* Contributions in Political Science, no. 365 (Westport, CT: Greenwood Press, 1996), 99-108, 184-85; and "Louisiana Lawyer," *Time,* February 24, 1936, 49-51.

19. Stern and Gressman, *Supreme Court Practice,* 62.

20. Ibid., 62, 70-71.

21. "Jurisdictional Statement," July 1963, folder 2, box 5753, U.S. Supreme Court Case Files, NARA, 4-9, 11-17, 24-27; and Phillip J. Cooper and Howard Ball, *The United States Supreme Court: From the Inside Out* (Upper Saddle River, NJ: Prentice Hall, 1996), 108-109.

22. *Chaplinsky v. New Hampshire,* 315 U.S. 568 (1942); and "Motion to Dismiss of Affirm on Behalf of the State of Louisiana," September 15, 1963, *Records and Briefs,* 7, 10-11, 13-18, 21, 30-31.

23. Docket Sheet, *"Jim Garrison v. Louisiana,"* undated, folder "Docket Books, October Term 1964," box 1328, William O. Douglas Papers, Manuscript Division, Library of Congress, Washington, D.C.; "Bar Group Moves for Reappraisal," *Times-Picayune,* November 9, 1963; and "High Court OK's Hearing for D.A.," *Times-Picayune,* November 13, 1963.

24. "Garrison Attacks Report by N.O. Bar Committee," *Times-Picayune,* November 15, 1963.

Chapter IV

1. Certiorari Memorandum from FXB [Francis X. Beytagh] to Earl Warren, November 1, 1963, folder "Conference Memos, Appellate No. 1-6, OT 1964," box 261, Earl Warren Papers, Manuscript Division, Library of Congress, Washington, D.C. [hereinafter cited as Warren Papers, LOC]; and Lee Epstein, Jeffrey A. Segal, Harold J. Spaeth, and Thomas G. Walker, *The Supreme Court Compendium: Data, Decisions, and Developments* (Washington, D.C.: Congressional Quarterly Inc., 1994), 60.

2. *New York Times v. Sullivan*, 376 U.S. 254 (1964); and *Garrison v. Louisiana*, 379 U.S. 64 (1964).

3. Certiorari Memorandum from FXB [Francis X. Beytagh] to Earl Warren, November 1, 1963, folder "Conference Memos, Appellate No. 1-6, OT 1964," box 261, Warren Papers, LOC; Bernard Schwartz, *Super Chief: Earl Warren and His Supreme Court* (New York: New York University Press, 1983), 68; *Schenck v. U.S.*, 249 U.S. 47 (1919); and *Beauharnais v. Illinois*, 343 U.S. 250 (1952).

4. Warren was not the only justice to follow the recommendation of his clerk to either grant or deny Garrison's appeal. At least four of the court's other members did the same, which was not extraordinary given the number of appeals the court considered each term. Justices simply did not have time to read and reflect on each case, and relied instead on their clerks to supply the appeals' constitutional questions and arguments. Of the five certiorari memorandums available to researchers, all five justices followed their aides' advice. Warren, Douglas, and Goldberg voted to grant Garrison's appeal, while justices Clark and Harlan wanted to deny review. Certiorari Memorandum from FXB [Francis X. Beytagh] to Earl Warren, November 1, 1963, Warren Papers, LOC; Francis X. Beytagh, "On Earl Warren's Retirement," *Michigan Law Review* 67 (December 1968): 1477-78; Certiorari Memorandum from ELS [Evan L. Schwab] to William O. Douglas, October 31, 1963, folder "*Garrison v. Louisiana*," box 1339, William O. Douglas Papers, Manuscript Division, Library of Congress, Washington, D.C. [hereinafter cited as Douglas Papers, LOC]; Certiorari Memorandum, "*Garrison v. State of Louisiana*," folder "Certiorari Memoranda, OT63," box II:21, Arthur J. Goldberg, Jr. Papers, Manuscript Division, Library of Congress, Washington, D.C. [hereinafter cited as Goldberg Papers, LOC]; Certiorari Memorandum from JLMcH [James L. McHugh] to Tom C. Clark, "*Garrison v. Louisiana*," November 4, 1963, folder 2,"Supreme Court Bench Memoranda OT64," box B200, Tom C. Clark Papers, Rare Books & Special Collections, Tarlton Law Library, University of Texas at Austin [hereinafter cited as Clark Papers, UT]; Certiorari Memorandum from Lloyd L. Weinreb to John Marshall Harlan II, "*Garrison v. Louisiana*," October 30, 1963, folder "*Garrison v. Louisiana*," box 217, John Marshall Harlan II Papers, Seeley G. Mudd Manuscript Library, Princeton University, Princeton, NJ [hereinafter cited as Harlan Papers, Princeton]; Schwartz, *Super Chief*, 65-68; Docket Sheet, "*Jim Garrison vs. Louisiana*," undated, folder "Docket Books, OT 1964," box 1328, Douglas Papers, LOC.

5. "Brief for Appellant," February 13, 1964, in United States Supreme Court, *Records and Briefs* (California, MD: Congressional Information Service, 1964), microfiche, 9-12, 27 [hereinafter cited as *Records and Briefs*].

6. Ibid., 34-42.

7. *Roth v. U.S.*, 354 U.S. 476 (1957), quoted in Thomas L. Tedford, *Freedom of Speech in the United States*, 3rd ed. (State College, PA: Strata Publishing, 1997), 130; "Justice Black and First Amendment 'Absolutes': A Public Interview," *New York University Law Review* 37 (June 1962): 552-53; and "Brief for Appellant," *Records and Briefs*, 43-45.

8. "Brief on Behalf of State of Louisiana, Appellee," March 9, 1964, *Records and Briefs*, 5-6, 9.

9. Ibid., 14-24; and Robert L. Stern and Eugene Gressman, *Supreme Court Practice*, 3rd ed. (Washington, D.C.: BNA Incorporated, 1962), 561.

10. "Brief on Behalf of State of Louisiana, Appellee," March 9, 1964, *Records and Briefs*, 24-38.

11. Ibid., 38-47; and *Chaplinsky v. New Hampshire*, 315 U.S. 568 (1942).

12. *New York Times v. Sullivan*, 257-65.

13. Ibid.; Thomas I. Emerson, *The System of Freedom of Expression* (New York: Random House, 1970): 520-21; and Tedford, *Freedom of Speech in the United States*, 87-88.

14. *New York Times v. Sullivan*, 270-75; and "Brief for Appellant," *Records and Briefs*, 19-20.

15. *New York Times v. Sullivan*, 279-80.

16. The U.S. Supreme Court's decision in *New York Times v. Sullivan* was unanimous, although two justices, Hugo L. Black and Arthur J. Goldberg Jr., issued concurring opinions that insisted the decision should have eradicated all state libel laws. Black maintained that an "unconditional right to say what one pleases about public affairs" was a minimal guarantee of the First Amendment. Goldberg argued that both the First and Fourteenth Amendments afforded the right to criticize official conduct "despite the harm which may flow from excesses and abuses." Both justices would assert

similar claims in concurring opinions in the *Garrison* case. Ibid., 297-98.

17. "Motion to Remove Case from Summary Calendar," from FXB [Francis X. Beytagh] to Earl Warren, March 18, 1964, folder "Conference Memos, Appellate No. 1-6, OT 1964," box 261, Warren Papers, LOC; Docket Sheet, "*Jim Garrison v. Louisiana*," undated, folder "Docket Books OT64," box 1328, Douglas Papers, LOC; and "Supplemental Brief for Appellant," 6 April 1964, *Records and Briefs*, 1-9.

18. "Supplemental Brief for Appellee," April 16, 1964, *Records and Briefs*, 1, 5-7, 9-10.

19. Ibid., 5-8, 19-20.

20. Anthony Lewis, *Make No Law: The Sullivan Case and the First Amendment* (New York: Random House, 1991), 128-29; and Stephen L. Wasby, Anthony D'Amato, and Rosemary Metrailer, "The Functions of Oral Argument in the U.S. Supreme Court," *Quarterly Journal of Speech* 62 (December 1976): 413-15.

21. Emphasis added.

22. Oral Arguments of *Garrison v. Louisiana*, April 22, 1964, Case #400, Record #267.512, Sound Recordings from the National Archives and Records Administration [hereinafter cited as Oral Arguments, *Garrison v. Louisiana*, April 22, 1964].

23. Ibid.; and *Louisiana Revised Statutes*, 14:49 (1950).

24. Under an agreement with the U.S. Supreme Court, the National Archives and Records Administration makes available to the public recordings of oral arguments but does not identify the voices of any of the justices. In instances where an attorney addresses a justice individually, or where it is obvious who is speaking, I have used the justice's name. Otherwise, to avoid misidentifying a court member, I have chosen not to attempt identification.

25. Oral Arguments, *Garrison v. Louisiana*, April 22, 1964.

26. Ibid.

27. Ibid.

28. Ibid.

29. Ibid; "Garrison Defamation Hearing Enables Justice to Unbend," *Washington Post*, April 23, 1964; and "Tribunal Hears Garrison Case," *New Orleans Times-Picayune*, April 23, 1964.

30. Oral Arguments, *Garrison v. Louisiana*, April 22, 1964.

31. Oral Arguments, *Garrison v. Louisiana*, April 22, 1964; "Garrison Defamation Hearing Enables Justice to Unbend," *Washington Post*, April 23, 1964; Liva Baker, *The Second Battle of New Orleans: The Hundred-Year Struggle to Integrate the Schools* (New York: HarperCollins, 1996), 355-57, 373-75; and J.W. Peltason, *Fifty-Eight Lonely Men: Southern Federal Judges and School Desegregation* (New York: Harcourt, Brace & World, 1961), 224-25, 227.

32. William O. Douglas, Conference Notes, "No. 400—*Garrison v. Louisiana*," April 24, 1964, folder "No. 4, *Garrison v. Louisiana*," box 1339, Douglas Papers, LOC; William J. Brennan, Jr., "Inside View of the High Court," *New York Times Magazine*, October 6, 1963, 100-102; and Tom C. Clark, "Inside the Court," in Alan F. Westin, ed., *The Supreme Court: Views from Inside* (New York: W.W. Norton, 1961), 45-48.

33. Douglas, Conference Notes, "No. 400—*Garrison v. Louisiana*," April 24, 1964, folder "No. 4, *Garrison v. Louisiana*," box 1339, Douglas Papers, LOC; and Assignment Sheet, "No. 400—*Garrison v. Louisiana*," undated, folder "Assignments OT63," box I:94, William J. Brennan, Jr. Papers, Library of Congress, Washington, D.C. [hereinafter cited as Brennan Papers, LOC].

34. Phillip J. Cooper and Howard Ball, *The United States Supreme Court: From the Inside Out* (Upper Saddle River, NJ: Prentice Hall, 1996), 198.

35. William J. Brennan, first draft, "No. 400—*Jim Garrison, Appellant, v. State of Louisiana*," [hereinafter cited as No. 400—*Garrison v. Louisiana*], May 16, 1964, 12-14, folder "No. 4—*Garrison v. Louisiana*," box 217, Harlan Papers, Princeton; and Circulation List, "No. 400—*Garrison v. Louisiana*," undated, folder 3, "October Term, 1963," box A211, Clark Papers, UT.

36. Memorandum from Potter Stewart to William Brennan, "Re: No. 400—*Garrison v. Louisiana*," May 19, 1964, folder "OT63—*Garrison v. Louisiana*," box I:111, Brennan Papers, LOC.

37. Tom C. Clark, "Memorandum to the Conference, Re: No. 400—*Garrison v. Louisiana*," May 20, 1964, and Tom C. Clark, first draft, No. 400—*Garrison v. Louisiana*, May 28, 1964, 1-8, both in folder "No. 4—*Garrison v. Louisiana*," box 217, Harlan Papers, Princeton.

38. Memorandum from John Marshall Harlan to Tom C. Clark, "Re: No. 400—*Garrison v. Louisiana*," June 1, 1964, folder 2, "No. 4—*Garrison v. Louisiana*, 1964 June," box A166, Clark Papers, UT; Clark, second draft, No. 400—*Garrison v. Louisiana*, June 2, 1964, 1, folder "No. 4—*Garrison v. Louisiana*," box 217, Harlan Papers, Princeton.

39. Brennan's second draft, which he circulated on May 21, 1964, contained only minor, stylistic changes.

40. Brennan, third draft, No. 400—*Garrison v. Louisiana*, June 2, 1964, 7, folder "No. 4—*Garrison v. Louisiana*," box 217, Harlan Papers, Princeton.

41. A justice writes a concurring opinion when he agrees with the outcome of an appeal, but for different reasons that those expressed in the majority opinion. A concurrence does not affect the final vote tally, however. For example, in *New York Times v. Sullivan*, justices Black, Douglas, and Goldberg each wrote concurring opinions, but the decision remained unanimous. Only a dissent affects unanimity. Elder Witt, ed., *The Supreme Court, A to Z: A Ready Reference Encyclopedia* (Washington, D.C: Congressional Quarterly, 1994), 97-98, 143, 280-82.

42. Brennan, first draft, No. 400—*Garrison v. Louisiana*, May 16, 1964, 7, and William O. Douglas, first draft, No. 400—*Garrison v. Louisiana*, June 2, 1964, 2-3, both in folder "No. 4—*Garrison v. Louisiana*," box 217, Harlan Papers, Princeton.

43. Clark, third draft, No. 400—*Garrison v. Louisiana*, June 4, 1964, 6, and Byron R. White, first draft, No. 400—*Garrison v. Louisiana*, June 10, 1964, 1-8, both in folder "No. 4—*Garrison v. Louisiana*," box 217, Harlan Papers, Princeton.

44. White, first draft, No. 400—*Garrison v. Louisiana*, June 10, 1964, 1-8, folder "No. 4—*Garrison v. Louisiana*," box 217, Harlan Papers, Princeton.

45. Memorandum from JLMcH [James L. McHugh] to Tom C. Clark, "Re: *Garrison v. Louisiana*," June 10, 1964, folder 2, "No. 4—*Garrison v. Louisiana*, 1964 June," box A166, Clark Papers, UT; Memorandum

from Hugo L. Black to William O. Douglas, June 13, 1964, folder "No. 400—*Garrison v. Louisiana*, OT63," box 1339, Douglas Papers, LOC; Memorandum from John Marshall Harlan to Tom C. Clark, "Re: No. 400—*Garrison v. Louisiana*," June 12, 1964, and Arthur J. Goldberg, Jr., draft, No. 400—*Garrison v. Louisiana*, May 19, 1964, 1, both in folder "No. 4—*Garrison v. Louisiana*," box 217, Harlan Papers, Princeton.

46. Order List, "Orders in Pending Cases," June 22, 1964, folder "Order Lists and Per Curium, OT 63," box I:96, Brennan Papers, LOC; and "Reargue Libel Case, Is Order," *Times-Picayune*, June 23, 1964.

Chapter V

1. Assignment Chart, "Assignment of Argued Cases for Opinion—October Term 1963," folder "Assignment Charts, October terms, 1952-1968," box 125, Earl Warren Papers, Library of Congress, Washington, D.C. [hereinafter cited as Warren Papers, LOC]; Bob Woodward and Scott Armstrong, *The Brethren: Inside the Supreme Court* (New York: Simon & Schuster, 1979), 64-65; and Phillip J. Cooper and Howard Ball, *The United States Supreme Court: From the Inside Out* (Upper Saddle River, NJ: Prentice Hall, 1996), 132.

2. *Garrison v. Louisiana*, 379 U.S. 64 (1964); Assignment Chart, "Assignment of Argued Cases for Opinion—October Term 1963," folder "Assignment Charts, October terms, 1952-1968," box 125, Warren Papers, LOC; and Circulation List, "No. 400—*Garrison v. Louisiana*," undated, folder 3, "October Term, 1963," box A211, Tom C. Clark Papers, Rare Books & Special Collections, Tarlton Law Library, University of Texas at Austin [hereinafter cited as Clark Papers, UT].

3. The defamation charges came after Cox's initial arrest for violating Louisiana statutes that governed disturbing the peace, obstructing public passages, and picketing near a courthouse. An East Baton Rouge Parish court found Cox guilty on the three charges, and the Louisiana Supreme Court affirmed the decision. Cox appealed to the U.S. Supreme Court, which heard oral arguments in the case the same week it reheard Garrison's appeal. In January 1965, the court overturned Cox's convictions in two landmark First Amendment decisions. The first, *Cox v. Louisiana I*, said Louisiana's peace disturbance statute, in its attempt to prevent public unrest, unfairly limited the right to assemble peaceably. The court held that the First Amendment protected and even invited dispute. The second case, *Cox v. Louisiana II*, overturned Cox's convictions for picketing near

the courthouse and obstructing public passages because Baton Rouge police had improperly applied the statute when they initially told Cox and the other protesters they were not picketing too close to the court building. However, the Supreme Court upheld the legality of both statutes, ruling that state governments have the right to prescribe some limitations as to where protesters could demonstrate. *Cox v. Louisiana*, 379 U.S. 536 and 379 U.S. 559 (1965); and Thomas L. Tedford, *Freedom of Speech in the United States*, 3d ed. (State College: PA: Strata Publishing, 1997), 260-61.

4. Oral Arguments of *Garrison v. Louisiana*, October 19, 1964, Case #4, Record #267.496, Sound Recordings from the National Archives and Records Administration [hereinafter cited as Oral Arguments, *Garrison v. Louisiana*, October 19, 1964].

5. Ibid.

6. Emphasis added. Ibid.

7. Ibid.

8. Ibid.; and Dennis J. Hutchinson, *The Man Who Once Was Whizzer White: A Portrait of Justice Byron R. White* (New York: Free Press, 1998), 332.

9. Louisiana Governor Earl K. Long once lampooned Gremillion's legal skills by saying, "If you want to lose anything real good, just put it in Jack Gremillion's law book." The attorney general's performance before the Supreme Court suggests that Long was correct. A.J. Liebling, *The Earl of Louisiana* (Baton Rouge: Louisiana State University Press, 1986), 161-62.

10. Oral Arguments, *Garrison v. Louisiana*, October 19, 1964.

11. Ibid.; *New York Times v. Sullivan*, 376 U.S. 250 (1964); and John M. Harlan, "The Role of Oral Argument," in Alan F. Westin, ed., *The Supreme Court: Views from Inside* (New York: W.W. Norton, 1961), 57-59.

12. Oral Arguments, *Garrison v. Louisiana*, October 19, 1964.

13. William J. Brennan, Conference Notes, "No. 4—*Garrison v. Louisiana*," October 23, 1964, folder "Dockets, OT64," box I:113, William J. Brennan, Jr. Papers, Library of Congress, Washington, D.C. [hereinafter cited as Brennan Papers, LOC]; Docket Sheet, "No. 4—*Jim Garrison v. Louisiana*," undated, folder "Dockets, OT64," box 379, Warren Papers, LOC;

William O. Douglas, Conference Notes, "No. 4—*Garrison v. Louisiana*," October 23, 1964, folder "No. 4—*Garrison v. Louisiana*," box 1339, William O. Douglas Papers, Library of Congress, Washington, D.C. [hereinafter cited as Douglas Papers, LOC]; and Conference List, "List 3, Sheet 1—For Conference, Friday, October 23, 1964, Argued and Submitted," folder 3, "Conference Lists, 1964 October-1965 February," box A164, Clark Papers, UT.

14. Conference List, "Miscellaneous Petition," October 23, 1964, folder "Conference Lists, OT64," box I:113, and Assignment List, "October Term, A.D. 1964," October 27, 1964, folder "Assignment Lists," box I:112, both in Brennan Papers, LOC.

15. William J. Brennan, first draft, "No. 4—*Jim Garrison, Appellant, v. State of Louisiana*," [hereinafter cited as No. 4—*Garrison v. Louisiana*], November 14, 1964, 4, 7, 10-11, folder "No. 4—*Garrison v. Louisiana*," box 217, John Marshall Harlan II Papers, Seeley G. Mudd Manuscript Library Princeton University, Princeton, NJ [hereinafter cited as Harlan Papers, Princeton].

16. Brennan, first draft, No. 4—*Garrison v. Louisiana*, November 14, 1964, 11-12, folder "No. 4—*Garrison v. Louisiana*," box 217, Harlan Papers, Princeton.

17. Ibid., 9, 13.

18. Brennan circulated a second draft on 16 November 1964, but it contained only minor stylistic changes.

19. Ibid., 15-16; Brennan, third draft, No. 4—*Garrison v. Louisiana*, November 18, 1964,15, folder "No. 4—*Garrison v. Louisiana*," box 217, Harlan Papers, Princeton; Tom C. Clark, handwritten note on Certiorari Memorandum, November 17, 1964, folder "Memoranda, OT64," box B200, Memorandum from WJB [William J. Brennan] to Mr. Justice Clark, Mr. Justice Harlan, Mr. Justice Stewart, and Mr. Justice White, November 19, 1964, folder 3, "No. 4—*Garrison v. Louisiana*, 1964 November & undated," box A166, both in Clark Papers, UT; and Memorandum from WJB to Paul [S. Paul Posner], November 19, 1964, Memorandum from Byron R. White to William J. Brennan, "Re: No. 4—*Garrison v. Louisiana*," November 19, 1964, and Memorandum from Potter Stewart to William J. Brennan, folder "Re: No. 4—*Garrison v. Louisiana*," November 19, 1964, all in folder "*Garrison v. Louisiana* Case File, OT64," box I:116, Brennan Papers, LOC.

20. William O. Douglas, early draft, No. 4—*Garrison v. Louisiana*, November 18, 1964, 2, folder "No. 4—*Garrison v. Louisiana*, Miscellaneous Memoranda, etc.," box 1339, Douglas Papers, LOC.

21. JSC [James S. Campbell] to William O. Douglas, Memoranda and Suggested Footnotes, November 19, 1964, folder "No. 4—*Garrison v. Louisiana*, Vote of Court and Law Clerks," box 1339, Douglas Papers, LOC; and Douglas, final draft, No. 4—*Garrison v. Louisiana*, November 21,1964, folder 3, "No. 4—*Garrison v. Louisiana*, 1964 November & undated," box A166, Clark Papers, UT.

22. Justices Black and Douglas issued separate concurring opinions, but also joined each other's concurrence. Hugo L. Black, first draft, No. 4—*Garrison v. Louisiana*, November 20, 1964, 1, and Black, final draft, No. 4—*Garrison v. Louisiana*, November 21, 1964, 1-2, both in folder "No. 4—*Garrison v. Louisiana*," box 217, Harlan Papers, Princeton; Hugo L. Black to William O. Douglas, November 18, 1964, folder "No. 4—*Garrison v. Louisiana*, Miscellaneous Memoranda, etc.," box 1339, Douglas Papers, LOC; and Black, second draft, No. 4—*Garrison v. Louisiana*, November 21, 1964, 1, folder 3, "No. 4—*Garrison v. Louisiana*, 1964 November & undated," box A166, Clark Papers, UT.

23. Brennan, No. 4—*Garrison v. Louisiana*, [labeled "What the Justice Delivered"], November 23, 1964, folder "*Garrison v. Louisiana* Case File, OT 64," box I:116, Brennan Papers, LOC; List, "Agenda for the Conference" November 20, 1964, folder "Conference Lists," box 148, and Agenda, "Court Calendar," November 23, 1964, folder "Agendas for the Court, OT 1961-1965," box 125, both in Warren Papers, LOC.

Conclusion

1. "Never Doubted Outcome in Appeal, Says Garrison," *New Orleans Times-Picayune*, November 24, 1964.

2. Rosemary James and Jack Wardlaw, *Plot or Politics? The Garrison Case and Its Cast* (New Orleans: Pelican Publishing, 1967), 22-24; Milton E. Brener, *The Garrison Case: A Study in the Abuse of Power* (New York: Clarkson E. Potter, 1969), 20; "Books Charges Refused by DA," *Times-Picayune*, June 19, 1963; "Citizens Group Raps Garrison," *Times-Picayune*, June 20, 1963; "Charges in City Court Readied," *Times-Picayune*, June 21, 1963; and "Schiro Endorses Arrest, Denounces Baldwin Book," *Times-Picayune*, June 25, 1963.

3. *Garrison v. Louisiana*, 379 U.S. 64 (1964).

4. *New York Times v. Sullivan*, 376 U.S. 250 (1964); Clifton O. Lawhorne, *The Supreme Court and Libel* (Carbondale: Southern Illinois University Press, 1981), 38; and Douglas S. Campbell, *The Supreme Court and the Mass Media: Selected Cases, Summaries, and Analyses* (New York: Praeger, 1990), 57.

5. Ronald L. Naquin, "Constitutional Law—Freedom of Speech—Defamation," *Tulane Law Review* 39 (February 1965): 356, 358; and *Garrison v. Louisiana*, 76-77.

6. *Garrison v. Louisiana*, 73-75, 78.

7. Clifton O. Lawhorne, *Defamation and Public Officials: The Evolving Law of Libel* (Carbondale: Southern Illinois University Press, 1971), 222-33; and *Garrison v. Louisiana*, 78-79.

8. *Beauharnais v. Illinois*, 343 U.S. 250 (1952); Thomas I. Emerson, *The System of Freedom of Expression* (New York: Random House, 1970), 396, 535-36; W. Wat Hopkins, *Actual Malice: Twenty-Five Years after Times v. Sullivan* (New York: Praeger, 1989), 29-30; Samuel G. McNamara, "Recent Developments Concerning Constitutional Limitations on State Defamation Laws," *Vanderbilt Law Review* 18 (June 1965): 1429, 1434-35, 1443-46; and James R. Conway, "Torts—Libel—Proof of Actual Malice," *Loyola Law Review* 13, no. 1 (1966): 211.

9. *Ashton v. Kentucky*, 384 U.S. 195 (1966); *Rosenblatt v. Baer*, 383 U.S. 75 (1966); *Curtis Publishing Co. v. Butts*, 388 U.S. 130 (1967); *Rosenbloom v. Metromedia*, 403 U.S. 29 (1971); *Monitor Patriot Co. v. Roy*, 401 U.S. 265 (1971); *Gertz v. Welch*, 418 U.S. 323 (1974); Lawhorne, *Defamation and Public Officials*, 222-25; Emerson, *The System of Freedom of Expression*, 390-91; Franklyn S. Haiman, *Speech and Law in a Free Society* (Chicago: University of Chicago Press, 1981), 44-46; Thomas L. Tedford, *Freedom of Speech in the United States*, 3rd ed. (State College, PA: Strata Publishing, 1997), 91-95; and Jerome A. Barron and C. Thomas Dienes, *Handbook of Free Speech and Free Press* (Boston: Little, Brown, 1979), 302-303, 305-306.

10. *Mangual v. Rotger-Sabat*, 317 F.3d 45, 56 (1st Cir. 2003); Media Law Resource Center, "Criminalizing Speech about Reputation: The Legacy of Criminal Libel in the U.S. after *Sullivan* & *Garrison*," *MLRC Bulletin*, no. 1 (March 2003), 11, 37; George E. Stevens, "Criminal Libel after *Garrison*,"

Journalism Quarterly 68 (Autumn 1991): 522-25; and John D. Stevens, Robert L. Bailey, Judith F. Krueger, and John M. Mollwitz, "Criminal Libel as Seditious Libel, 1916-65." *Journalism Quarterly* 43 (Spring 1966): 110-12.

11. In 1968, the Louisiana Legislature reduced the punishment for defamation from a maximum fine of $3,000, one year in jail, or both, to a maximum fine of $500, six months in jail, or both. The 1968 measure is the only time legislators have revisited the state's defamation law since the Supreme Court's *Garrison v. Louisiana* decision. *Acts of the Louisiana Legislature*, 647:1 (1968).

12. The jurisdictions with criminal defamation laws written prior to the *Garrison* decision include Colorado, Florida, Idaho, Kansas, Louisiana, Michigan, Minnesota, Montana, New Hampshire, New Mexico, North Carolina, North Dakota, Oklahoma, Utah, Virginia, Washington, Wisconsin, Puerto Rico, and the Virgin Islands. After *Garrison*, the criminal libel laws of thirty-three states were either revised by legislatures or struck down by courts. Media Law Resource Center, "Criminalizing Speech about Reputation," *MLRC Bulletin*, 15; Lawhorne, *Defamation and Public Officials*, 214; *Louisiana Revised Statutes*, 14:47-14:50 (2006); *Snyder v. Ware*, 314 F.Supp. 335, affirmed 90 S.Ct. 1355, 367 U.S. 589 (1970); *State v. Snyder*, 277 So.2d 660 (1973); Michael A. Konczal, "The Development of Defamation Law in Louisiana, 1800-1988" (Master's thesis, University of Southwestern Louisiana, 1988), 37-42, 162-64; and Naquin, "Constitutional Law—Freedom of Speech—Defamation," *Tulane Law Review*, 356.

13. David Chandler, "The Devil's D.A.," *New Orleans*, November 1966, 90; and John Pope, "JFK Case Put DA on World Stage," *Times-Picayune*, October 22, 1992, A1, A10.

14. Although Garrison's memoir does not mention *Garrison v. Louisiana*, the ruling did receive a passing reference in the film *JFK*. Garrison, played by Kevin Costner, is meeting with lawyer Dean Andrews (John Candy), who is dodging the district attorney's questions about the identity of the mysterious "Clay Bertrand," which Garrison would later claim was Clay Shaw's alias. Frustrated by Andrew's cagey answers, Garrison shouts: "I took nine [sic] judges on, Deano, right here in New Orleans, and I beat 'em all." Oliver Stone and Zachary Sklar, *JFK: The Book of the Film* (New York: Applause Books, 1992), 65.

15. Pope, "JFK Case Put DA on World Stage," *Times-Picayune*, October

22, 1992, A10; Edward Jay Epstein, "Shots in the Dark," *New Yorker*, November 30, 1992, 48; Bruce Lambert, "Jim Garrison, 70, Theorized on Kennedy Death, Dies," *New York Times*, October 22, 1992, B12; and J.Y. Smith, "La. Judge Jim Garrison Dies; 'JFK' Film Based on His Ideas," *Washington Post*, October 22, 1992, B6.

16. *Garrison v. Louisiana*, 74-75.

Bibliography

Primary Sources

<u>Manuscript Collections</u>:

Manuscript Division, Library of Congress, Washington, D.C.
 Hugo Lafayette Black Papers
 William J. Brennan Jr. Papers
 William O. Douglas Papers
 Arthur J. Goldberg Jr. Papers
 Earl Warren Papers

Louisiana and Lower Mississippi Valley Collections, Louisiana State
 University, Baton Rouge.
 Mss. 2558, John B. Fournet Papers

National Archives and Records Administration, College Park, MD.
 Record Group 541, President John F. Kennedy Assassination
 Records Collection
 Papers of Jim Garrison
 Records of the New Orleans Metropolitan Crime
 Commission

National Archives and Records Administration, Washington, D.C.
 Record Group 267, Records of the United States Supreme Court

Rare Books & Special Collections, Tarlton Law Library, University
 of Texas at Austin
 Tom C. Clark Papers

Seeley G. Mudd Manuscript Library, Princeton University
 John Marshall Harlan II Papers

<u>Judicial Records</u>:

Ashton v. Kentucky. 384 U.S. 195 (1966).

Beauharnais v. Illinois. 343 U.S. 250 (1952).

Chaplinsky v. New Hampshire. 315 U.S. 568 (1942).

Cox v. Louisiana. 379 U.S. 536, 379 U.S. 559 (1965).

Curtis Publishing Co. v. Butts. 388 U.S. 130 (1967).

Garrison v. Louisiana. 379 U.S. 64 (1964).

Gertz v. Welch. 418 U.S. 323 (1974).

Grosjean v. American Press Co. 297 U.S. 233 (1936).

Mangual v. Rotger-Sabat. 317 F.3d 45, 56 (1st Cir. 2003).

Moity v. Louisiana. 379 U.S. 201 (1964).

Monitor Patriot Co. v. Roy. 401 U.S. 265 (1971).

New York Times v. Sullivan. 376 U.S. 250 (1964).

Oral Arguments of Garrison v. Louisiana, 22 April 1964. Case #400, Record #267.512. Sound Recordings from the National Archives and Records Administration.

Oral Arguments of Garrison v. Louisiana, 19 October 1964. Case #4, Record #267.496. Sound Recordings from the National Archives and Records Administration.

Rosenblatt v. Baer. 383 U.S. 75 (1966).

Rosenbloom v. Metromedia. 403 U.S. 29 (1971).

Schenck v. U.S. 249 U.S. 47 (1919).

Snyder v. Ware. 314 F.Supp. 335, affirmed 90 S.Ct. 1355, 367 U.S. 589 (1970).

State of Louisiana v. Jim Garrison. 244 La. 787 (1963).

State of Louisiana v. Jim Garrison. Files of the Orleans Parish Criminal District Court, New Orleans. Microfilm.

State of Louisiana v. Jim Garrison. Office of the Clerk of Court, Supreme Court of Louisiana, New Orleans. Microfilm.

State of Louisiana v. Snyder. 277 So.2nd 660 (1973).

United States Supreme Court. *Records and Briefs.* California, MD: Congressional Information Service, 1964. Microfiche.

Legislative Records:

Acts of the Louisiana Legislature.

Louisiana Revised Statutes.

Newspapers:

New Orleans Times-Picayune.

New York Times.

Wardlaw, Jack. "A Crusading DA and His Eight Foes: The Judges." *National Observer.* 28 January 1963, 3.

Washington Post.

Other Printed Primary Sources:

Bartholomew, Paul C. "The Supreme Court of the United States, 1964-1965." *Western Political Quarterly* 18 (December 1965): 741-754.

Beytagh, Francis X. "On Earl Warren's Retirement." *Michigan Law Review* 67 (December 1968): 1477-92.

Black, Hugo LaFayette. *A Constitutional Faith.* New York: Alfred A. Knopf, 1969.

Brener, Milton E. *The Garrison Case: A Study in the Abuse of Power.* New York: Clarkson N. Potter, 1969.

Brennan, William J., Jr. "Inside View of the High Court." *New York Times Magazine*, 6 October 1963, 35, 100-103.

_____. *My Affair with Freedom: A Collection of His Opinions and Speeches Drawn from His First Decade as a United States Supreme Court Justice.* Edited by Stephen J. Friedman. New York: Antheum, 1967.

_____. "The Supreme Court and the Meiklejohn Interpretation of the First Amendment." *Harvard Law Review* 79 (November 1965): 1-20.

"Case of the Crusading DA." *Newsweek*, 18 February 1963, 26.

Chafee, Zechariah, Jr. *Free Speech in the United States.* Cambridge, MA: Harvard University Press, 1946.

Chandler, David. "The Devil's D.A." *New Orleans*, November 1966, 31-32, 90-91.

Clark, Tom C. "Internal Operation of the United States Supreme Court." *Journal of the American Judicature Society* 13 (August 1959): 45-51.

Conway, James R., III. "Torts—Libel—Proof of Actual Malice." *Loyola Law Review* 13, no. 1 (1966): 208-13.

Deutsch, Eberhard P. "From Zenger to Garrison: A Tale of Two Centuries." *New York State Bar Journal* 38 (October 1966): 409-19.

Douglas, William O. *The Court Years, 1939-1975: The Autobiography of William O. Douglas.* New York: Random House, 1980.

Epstein, Edward Jay. "Shots in the Dark." *New Yorker*, 30 November 1992, 47-58.

Frugé, J. Cleveland. *Biographies of Louisiana Judges.* n.p: Louisiana District Judges Association, 1961.

_____. *Biographies of Louisiana Judges.* n.p: Louisiana District

Judges Association, 1965.

Garrison, Jim. *A Heritage of Stone*. New York: G.P. Putnam's Sons, 1970.

_____. *On the Trail of the Assassins: My Investigation and Prosecution of the Murder of President Kennedy*. New York: Sheridan Square Press, 1988.

_____. *The Star Spangled Contract*. New York: McGraw-Hill, 1976.

Goldberg, Arthur J. *The Defenses of Freedom: The Public Papers of Arthur J. Goldberg*. New York: Harper & Row, 1966.

_____. "Mr. Justice Brennan and the First Amendment." *Rutgers Camden Law Journal* 4 (Fall 1972): 8-43.

James, Rosemary, and Jack Wardlaw. *Plot or Politics? The Garrison Case and Its Cast*. New Orleans: Pelican Publishing House, 1967.

"Justice Black and First Amendment 'Absolutes': A Public Interview." *New York University Law Review* 37 (June 1962): 549-63.

Lewis, Anthony. "Justice Black at 75: Still the Dissenter." *New York Times Magazine*, 26 February 1961, 13, 73-75.

_____. "A Man Born to Act, Not to Muse." *New York Times Magazine*, 30 June 1968, 9, 46-50.

_____. "A Talk with Warren on Crime, the Court, the Country." *New York Times Magazine*, 19 October 1969, 34, 122-36.

"Louisiana Lawyer." *Time*, 24 February 1936, 49-51.

McNamara, Samuel G. "Recent Developments Concerning Constitutional Limitations on State Defamation Laws." *Vanderbilt Law Review* 18 (June 1965): 1429-55.

Naquin, Ronald L. "Constitutional Law—Freedom of Speech—Defamation." *Tulane Law Review* 39 (February 1965): 355-62.

Phelan, James. "Vice Man Cometh." *Saturday Evening Post,* 8 June 1963, 67-71.

Roberts, Gene. "The Case of Jim Garrison and Lee Oswald." *New York Times Magazine,* 21 May 1967, 32-40.

Rodell, Fred. "It is the Earl Warren Court." *New York Times Magazine,* 13 March 1966, 92-100.

Stern, Robert L., and Eugene Gressman. *Supreme Court Practice,* 3rd ed. Washington, D.C.: BNA Incorporated, 1962.

Stewart, Potter. "Reflections on the Supreme Court." *Litigation* 8 (Spring 1982): 8-13.

"The Supreme Court, 1964 Term." *Harvard Law Review* 79 (November 1965): 56-206.

Warren, Earl. *The Memoirs of Chief Justice Earl Warren.* New York: Doubleday, 1977.

Westin, Alan F. *The Supreme Court: An Autobiography.* New York: MacMillian, 1963.

_____, ed. *The Supreme Court: Views from Inside.* New York: W.W. Norton, 1961.

Secondary Sources

Anderson, David A. "Origins of the Press Clause." *UCLA Law Review* 30 (February 1983): 456-541. Available from LexisNexis Academic.

Angoff, Charles. *The Book of Libel.* New York: Essential Books, 1946. Reprint, New York: A.S. Barnes, 1966.

Baker, C. Edwin. *Human Liberty and Freedom of Speech.* New York: Oxford University Press, 1989.

Baker, Liva. *The Second Battle of New Orleans: The Hundred-Year*

Struggle to Integrate the Schools. New York: HarperCollins, 1996.

Ball, Howard. *Hugo Black: Cold Steel Warrior.* New York: Oxford University Press, 1996.

_____. *The Vision and Dream of Justice Hugo L. Black: An Examination of a Judicial Philosophy.* University: University of Alabama Press, 1975.

Ball, Howard, and Phillip J. Cooper. *Of Power and Right: Hugo Black, William O. Douglas, and America's Constitutional Revolution.* New York: Oxford University Press, 1992.

Barron, Jerome A., and C. Thomas Dienes. *Handbook of Free Speech and Free Press.* Boston: Little, Brown, 1979.

Baum, Lawrence. *The Supreme Court.* 2nd ed. Washington, D.C.: Congressional Quarterly, 1985.

Billings, Warren M. "The Supreme Court of Louisiana and the Administration of Justice, 1813-1995." *Louisiana History* 37 (Fall 1996): 389-404.

Biskupic, Joan, and Elder Witt. *The Supreme Court at Work.* 2nd ed. Washington, D.C.: Congressional Quarterly, 1997.

Bogen, David S. *Bulwark of Liberty: The Court and the First Amendment.* Port Washington, NY: Associated Faculty Press, 1984.

Brant, Irving. "Seditious Libel: Myth and Reality." *New York University Law Review* 39 (January 1964): 1-19.

Campbell, Douglas S. *The Supreme Court and the Mass Media: Selected Cases, Summaries, and Analyses.* New York: Praeger, 1990.

Cooper, Phillip J., and Howard Ball. *The United States Supreme Court: From the Inside Out.* Upper Saddle River, N.J.: Prentice Hall, 1996.

Cortner, Richard C. *The Kingfish and the Constitution: Huey Long, the First Amendment, and the Emergence of Modern Press Freedom in*

America. Contributions in Political Science, no. 365. Westport, CT: Greenwood Press, 1996.

Cox, Archibald. *The Warren Court: Constitutional Decision as an Instrument of Reform.* Cambridge, Mass.: Harvard University Press, 1968.

Dennis, Everette E., Donald M. Gillmor, and David L. Grey, ed. *Justice Hugo Black and the First Amendment.* Ames: Iowa State University Press, 1978.

Dickson, Del. *The Supreme Court in Conference, 1940-1985: The Private Discussions behind Nearly 300 Supreme Court Decisions.* New York: Oxford University Press, 2001.

DiEugenio, James. *Destiny Betrayed: JFK, Cuba, and the Garrison Case.* New York: Sheridan Square Press, 1992.

Dorsen, Norman. "The Second Mr. Justice Harlan: A Constitutional Conservative." *New York University Law Review* 44 (April 1969): 249-71.

Dunne, Gerald T. *Hugo Black and the Judicial Revolution.* New York: Simon & Schuster, 1977.

Duram, James C. *Justice William O. Douglas.* Twayne's United States Authors Series, ed. Warren French. Boston: Twayne Publishers, 1981.

Eisler, Kim Issac. *A Justice for All: William J. Brennan, Jr., and the Decisions that Transformed America.* New York: Simon & Schuster, 1993.

Emerson, Thomas I. *The System of Freedom of Expression.* New York: Random House, 1970.

_____. *Toward a General Theory of the First Amendment.* New York: Random House, 1966.

Emerson, Thomas I., David Haber, and Norman Dorsen. *Political and*

Civil Rights in the United States, 2 vols. Boston: Little, Brown and Co., 1967.

Epstein, Edward Jay. *Counterplot*. New York: Viking Press, 1969.

Epstein, Lee, Jeffrey A. Segal, Harold J. Spaeth, and Thomas G. Walker. *The Supreme Court Compendium: Data, Decisions, and Developments*. Washington, D.C.: Congressional Quarterly Inc., 1994.

Flammonde, Paris. *The Kennedy Conspiracy: An Uncommissioned Report on the Jim Garrison Investigation*. New York: Meredith Press, 1969.

Freyer, Tony. *Hugo L. Black and the Dilemma of American Liberalism*. Library of American Biography, ed. Oscar Handlin. Glenville, Ill.: Scott, Foresman, 1990.

Gambill, Joel Thirlo. "Hugo Black: The First Amendment and the Mass Media." Ph.D. diss., Southern Illinois University, 1973.

Gillmor, Donald M., and Jerome A. Barron. *Mass Communication Law: Cases and Comment*. American Casebook Series, ed. Jesse H. Choper, et al. St. Paul, MN: West Publishing, 1969.

Goldman, Roger L. *Justice William J. Brennan, Jr.: Freedom First*. New York: Carroll & Graf, 1994.

Graber, Mark A. *Transforming Free Speech: The Ambiguous Legacy of Civil Libertarianism*. Berkeley: University of California Press, 1991.

Haiman, Franklyn S. *Freedom of Speech*. To Protect These Rights, ed. Franklyn S. Haiman. Skokie, Ill.: National Textbook Co., 1976.

_____. *Speech and Law in a Free Society*. Chicago: University of Chicago Press, 1981.

Hall, Melinda Gann. "Electoral Politics and Strategic Voting in State Supreme Courts." *Journal of Politics* 54 (May 1992): 427-46.

Hemmer, Joseph J., Jr. *Communication under Law.* Vol.1, *Free Speech.* Metuchen, NJ: Scarecrow Press, 1979.

Hutchinson, Dennis J. *The Man Who Once Was Whizzer White: A Portrait of Justice Byron R. White.* New York: Free Press, 1998.

Hopkins, W. Wat. *Actual Malice: Twenty-Five Years after* Times v. Sullivan. New York: Praeger, 1989.

_____. *Mr. Justice Brennan and Freedom of Expression.* New York: Praeger, 1991.

Kalven, Harry. "'Uninhibited, Robust, and Wide-Open:' A Note on Free Speech and the Warren Court." *Michigan Law Review* 67 (December 1968): 289-302.

_____. *A Worthy Tradition: Freedom of Speech in America.* New York: Harper & Row, 1988.

Kelly, Alfred H. "Constitutional Liberty and the Law of Libel: A Historian's View." *American Historical Review* 74 (December 1968): 429-52.

Kirkwood, James. *American Grotesque: An Account of the Clay Shaw-Jim Garrison Affair in the City of New Orleans.* New York: Simon & Schuster, 1970.

Konczal, Michael A. "The Development of Defamation Law in Louisiana, 1800-1988." Master's thesis, University of Southwestern Louisiana, 1988.

Lambert, Patricia. *False Witness: The Real Story of Jim Garrison's Investigation and Oliver Stone's Film* JFK. New York: M. Evans, 1998.

Lawhorne, Clifton O. *Defamation and Public Officials: The Evolving Law of Libel.* Carbondale: Southern Illinois University Press, 1971.

_____. *The Supreme Court and Libel.* Carbondale: Southern

Illinois University Press, 1981.

Levy, Leonard W. *Emergence of a Free Press*. Chicago: Ivan R. Dee, 1985.

_____, ed. *Judicial Review and the Supreme Court*. New York: Harper Torchbooks, 1967.

Lewin, Nathan. "Justice Harlan: 'The Full Measure of the Man.'" *American Bar Association Journal* 58 (June 1972): 579-83.

Lewis, Anthony. *Make No Law: The Sullivan Case and the First Amendment*. New York: Vintage Books, 1992.

Liebling, A.J. *The Earl of Louisiana*. Baton Rouge: Louisiana State University Press, 1986.

Lisby, Gregory C. "No Place in the Law: The Ignominy of Criminal Libel in American Jurisprudence." *Communication Law and Policy* 9 (Autumn 2004): 433-87.

Marion, David E. *The Jurisprudence of Justice William J. Brennan, Jr.: The Law and Politics of Libertarian Dignity*. Lanham, MD: Rowman & Littlefield, 1997.

Matthews, Douglas R. "American Defamation Law: From *Sullivan*, through *Greenmoss*, and Beyond." *Ohio State Law Journal* 48 (Spring 1987): 513-32.

Media Law Resource Center. "Criminalizing Speech about Reputation: The Legacy of Criminal Libel in the U.S. after *Sullivan* & *Garrison*." *MLRC Bulletin*, no. 1 (March 2003): 1-155.

Mellen, Joan. *A Farewell to Justice: Jim Garrison, JFK's Assassination, and the Case that Should Have Changed History*. Dulles, VA: Potomac Books, 2005.

_____. *Jim Garrison: His Life and Time—The Early Years*. Southlake, Texas: JFK Lancer, 2008.

Mertz, Neil. "Constitutional Limitations on Libel Actions." *Baylor*

Law Review 28 (Winter 1976): 79-108.

Minnick, Wayne C. "The United States Supreme Court on Libel." *Quarterly Journal of Speech* 68 (Winter 1982): 384-96.

Murphy, Bruce Allen. *Wild Bill: The Legend and Life of William O. Douglas.* New York: Random House, 2003.

Nelson, Harold L., and Dwight L. Teeter Jr. *Law of Mass Communications: Freedom and Control of Print and Broadcast Media.* 4th ed. Mineola, NY: The Foundation Press, 1982.

Newman, Roger K. *Hugo Black: A Biography.* New York: Pantheon Books, 1994.

O'Brien, David M. *Storm Center: The Supreme Court in American Politics.* 2nd ed. New York: W.W. Norton: 1990.

Peltason, J.W. *Fifty-Eight Lonely Men: Southern Federal Judges and School Desegregation.* New York: Harcourt, Brace & World, 1961.

Peppers, Todd C. *Courtiers of the Marble Palace: The Rise and Influence of the Supreme Court Law Clerk.* Stanford, CA: Stanford University Press, 2006.

Perry, H.W., Jr. *Deciding to Decide: Agenda Setting in the United States Supreme Court.* Cambridge, MA: Harvard University Press, 1991.

Powe, L.A., Jr. "Evolution to Absolutism: Justice Douglas and the First Amendment." *Columbia Law Review* 74 (April 1974): 371-411.

Presser, Stephen B., and Jamil S. Zainaldin. *Law and Jurisprudence in American History: Cases and Comment.* 4th ed. American Casebook Series, ed. Jesse H. Choper, et al. St. Paul, MN: West Group, 2000.

Provine, Doris Marie. *Case Selection in the United States Supreme Court.* Chicago: University of Chicago Press, 1980.

Richards, Robert D. *Uninhibited, Robust, and Wide Open: Mr. Justice*

Brennan's Legacy to the First Amendment. Boone, NC: Parkway Publishers, 1994.

Rosenberg, Norman L. *Protecting the Best Men: An Interpretive History of the Law of Libel.* Studies in Legal History, ed. G. Edward White. Chapel Hill: University of North Carolina Press, 1986.

Rotunda, Ronald, ed. *Six Justices on Civil Rights.* New York: Oceana Publications, 1983.

Sack, Robert D. *Libel, Slander, and Related Problems.* 2nd ed. New York: Practising Law Institute, 1980.

Sanford, Bruce W. *Libel and Privacy: The Prevention and Defense of Litigation.* Clifton, NJ: Harcourt Brace Jovanovich, 1985.

Sayler, Richard H., Barry B. Boyer, and Richard E. Gooding, Jr., ed. *The Warren Court: A Critical Analysis.* New York: Chelsea House, 1969.

Schwartz, Bernard. *Decision: How the Supreme Court Decides Cases.* New York: Oxford University Press, 1996.

_____. *A History of the Supreme Court.* New York: Oxford University Press, 1993.

_____. *Super Chief: Earl Warren and His Supreme Court.* New York: New York University Press, 1983.

_____. *The Warren Court: A Retrospective.* New York: Oxford University Press, 1996.

Schwartz, Bernard, with Stephan Lesher. *Inside the Warren Court, 1953-1969.* Garden City, NJ: Doubleday, 1983.

Simon, James F. *Independent Journey: The Life of William O. Douglas.* New York: Harper & Row, 1980.

Smolla, Rodney A. *Law of Defamation.* 2nd ed. St. Paul, MN: West Group, 1992.

Souther, J. Mark. *New Orleans on Parade: Tourism and the Transformation of the Crescent City*. Baton Rouge: Louisiana State University Press, 2006.

Stevens, George E. "Criminal Libel after *Garrison*." *Journalism Quarterly* 68 (Autumn 1991): 522-27.

Stevens, John D., Robert L. Bailey, Judith F. Krueger, and John M. Mollwitz. "Criminal Libel as Seditious Libel, 1916-65." *Journalism Quarterly* 43 (Spring 1966): 110-13.

Stone, Oliver, and Zachary Sklar. JFK: *The Book of the Film*. New York: Applause Books, 1992.

Tedford, Thomas L. *Freedom of Speech in the United States*. 3rd ed. State College, PA: Strata Publishing, 1997.

Thompson, Dennis L. "The Kennedy Court: Left and Right of Center." *Western Political Quarterly* 26 (June 1973): 263-79.

Tushnet, Mark, ed. *The Warren Court in Historical and Political Perspective*. Charlottesville: University of Virginia Press, 1993.

Wasby, Stephen L., Anthony D'Amato, and Rosemary Metrailer. "The Functions of Oral Argument in the U.S. Supreme Court." *Quarterly Journal of Speech* 62 (December 1976): 410-22.

White, G. Edward. *Earl Warren: A Public Life*. New York: Oxford University Press, 1982.

Wiltz, Christine. *The Last Madam: A Life in the New Orleans Underworld*. New York: Da Capo Press, 2000.

Witt, Elder, ed. *The Supreme Court, A to Z: A Ready Reference Encyclopedia*. Washington, D.C: Congressional Quarterly, 1994.

Woodward, Bob, and Scott Armstrong. *The Brethren: Inside the Supreme Court*. New York: Simon & Schuster, 1979.

Yarbrough, Tinsley E. *John Marshall Harlan: Great Dissenter of the Warren Court*. New York: Oxford University Press, 1992.

Index

James Savage is a former newspaper editor and writer who earned his Master's degree in history from the University of Louisiana at Lafayette in 2006. He is the recipient of the Louisiana Historical Association's 2006 Hugh F. Rankin Prize and the Conference of Southern Graduate School's 2009 Master's Thesis Award. He is pursuing a Ph.D. in history at the University of Kentucky and lives in Lexington, Kentucky.